JOHN KEBLE

Priest, Professor and Poet

JOHN KEBLE

Priest, Professor and Poet

BRIAN W. MARTIN

CROOM HELM LONDON

Croom Helm Ltd.
2-10 St John's Road, London SW11

ISBN 0-085664-381-5

Printed and bound in Great Britain
by Redwood Burn Ltd, Trowbridge and Esher

Contents

Preface

John Keble's religious beliefs influenced his living. Whatever he did, or wrote, was in accord with his religious convictions. It is therefore necessary to define his religious thought in order to appreciate him as a poet. At the same time, it is essential to understand his aesthetic ideas, and since as Professor of Poetry at Oxford between 1832 and 1841 he made important pronouncements in the field of poetic criticism — perhaps the most important in the nineteenth century apart from S.T. Coleridge's and Matthew Arnold's — his theory of poetry should be examined. In this way of coming to terms with John Keble, it will be possible to establish his proper place as a literary figure in the nineteenth century.

This work will seek to do this, firstly by determining the nature of his Christian thought; secondly, by studying his theory of poetry; and lastly by considering their relationship to his poetry, especially *The Christian Year*.

I am indebted to the Warden and Fellows of Keble College, Oxford, for allowing me to use their library, John Keble's personal papers and unpublished correspondence, and John Keble's library which is still very largely intact. Mr M.B. Parkes has been particularly helpful. I am also grateful to the Reverend Canon Edward Keble for allowing me to use John Keble's letters which belong to him and are now deposited in Lambeth Palace Library. Professor P.A.W. Collins, Director of the Victorian Studies Centre in the University of Leicester, Dr Isobel Armstrong of Leicester University, and Professor Peter Marsh of Syracuse University, have all given enormous help and advice during various stages in the preparation of this work.

PART I

John Keble's Religious Thought

CHAPTER 1

The Universal Church

That the Catholic Church was really one, in spite of minor
and external difficulties in no case affecting the faith of the
Creeds, was, in one way or another, the corner-stone of the
entire fabric of Keble's thought.[1]

The enduring nature of the Church, which Keble considered to
be the living Body of Christ, its universality, and its catholicity
— *quod semper, quod ubique, quod ab omnibus* — were
fundamental ideas which Keble's writings and preachings were
always based on; and if those writings touched on other
matters they continually returned to rest firmly on the one idea
of the Church's catholicity. The sure theme, the steady rock is
seen in his early work, whether in parochial sermons or the
poetry of *The Christian Year,* or in his later work as seen in the
Tracts, or in his preface to the edition of Hooker's *Laws of
Ecclesiastical Polity* (1836), in his sermon on *Primitive
Tradition recognized in Holy Scripture* (1836), or in his sermon
on *Eucharistical Adoration* (1857).

The Church of England and the Church of Rome, he
considered, were parts of one Church: the differences between
the two were minor and external. Keble wrote a letter to his
brother in 1838 which dealt with some of the doubts people were
beginning to feel about John Henry Newman's drift: he wrote,

If it were not for you and Isaac [Williams], I should not be
made uneasy by the objections, but should account for
them by supposing that people do not realize the fact that
the three Churches are really one, though divided
externally.[2]

And he wrote to Dr Pusey in 1836, 'We agree with Rome about
our major premises, our differences are about the minor.'
Nevertheless, some of the premises which Keble considered
minor, and some of the externals to which he gave little

11

importance, others regarded in a far more serious light. The Bishop of Winchester, for instance, in 1841 refused to admit Peter Young, Keble's curate at Hursley, to Priest's Orders. Bishop Sumner considered Young's opinions about the doctrine of the Real Presence as unsound, and Keble interpreted his action as an indirect attack on himself. For some time Keble was at a loss to know how to take up the challenge. He consulted his friends, and wrote to his brother Thomas, all the time wary of offending episcopal authority, 'Remember, it is a case of quasi-heresy — which always suspends a Bishop's right to be obeyed.' But to Bishop Sumner he wrote in more appealing terms:

> I feel as if the present moment were of that critical kind in which it becomes every priest, even of the second order, to continue at his post, and do what trifle he can to sustain that Catholic interpretation of the English Formularies on which, from the bottom of my heart, I believe that our very being as a Church depends.[3]

Such was Keble's 'cri de coeur', and if Sumner had hoped for Keble's resignation, he was disappointed: it was the priest's duty to remain steadfast and make firm the bulwarks from within.

It was **also** a matter for great regret when Keble's friends censored **three** of the poems which he proposed to include in *Lyra Innocentium*. It was a critical time: Keble and his friends had before them the certain prospect that Newman would renounce the Church of England and embrace the Church of Rome. It was undoubtedly one of the heaviest sorrows of Keble's life, and he wondered what could be done to prepare the world for the news. In writing to his old friend, Sir John Coleridge, on 26 May 1845, Keble posed the problem and hoped that some of the ablest minds in the Church of England would be ready to defend the faith:

> Did I tell you that Pusey wrote some time since to ask whether one could think of anything to be done by way of preparation for the blow. Does anything occur to you? I wish P. himself, Moberly, Marriott, and Manning, etc., to apply themselves to the study of the controversy, for I am sure there will be great need of them.[4]

In view of this storm brewing for the calm of the Church of England both Charles Dyson[5] and Sir John Coleridge, realising the possibility of troubles that lay ahead, objected to the inclusion of some poems proposed for the *Lyra*; and the one poem which they especially censored was 'Mother out of Sight'. In his *Memoir* of Keble first published in 1868, Coleridge thought it the honest duty of a biographer of John Keble to publish the poem 'even if it might have been harmful originally'. Times had changed: Newman's defection was at some years' distance. Coleridge wrote that in 1868 '... it can do no harm, and may help to establish that legitimate, and as I believe, Scriptural reverence which is due to the object of it'.

But at the time Keble was disappointed and protested against Dyson's and Coleridge's decision in a letter written to Coleridge on 18 June 1845. In the first part of the letter he was businesslike in leaving the commercial arrangements for *Lyra Innocentium* in their hands: it is obvious from Keble's personal correspondence with his brother Thomas that he had a sound financial judgement, a fact often overlooked when Keble is talked of only in terms of a man of piety. There followed in the letter a degree of marked distress that the Dyson women, whom he took to be more representative of the Church of England at large than Dyson or Coleridge, objected too:

My Dear Coleridge,
You may believe that as far as trade is concerned, your opinion and Dyson's is very welcome to me, and I am quite willing to make the bargain with Parker which you may think equitable. I of course rather expected that some would demur to the things which you mention, and indeed I selected on purpose the three which I thought most likely to attract such objections as part of the specimen. But to say the truth, I did not expect that Mrs. and Miss Dyson would have objected on their own account; and it makes me even sadder than I was before, as shewing how very very far even the purest specimens of the English Church are from the *Whole Church* everywhere else. You see when I recommend the Ave, I mean merely the Scriptural part; but if such persons have this feeling, I suppose even this must be given up. With regard to the verse

'*He* calls thee Mother evermore';
if the Gospel is His word, and if the Gospel calls her His
Mother, and if the doctrinal decisions of the Whole
Church are His words, and if they call her Θεοτόκος,[6]
how can it be other than true, and so true, that to deny or
doubt it is touching a very vital part of the Faith.
Indeed, when I think of it, I am sure I must misunderstand
your objections; would it be removed if the words 'owns'
were put for 'calls'. This, however, I only ask for my own
satisfaction, for I see that it is quite impossible to print
those verses in the face of such a feeling as you express on
the part of the Dysons, and I cannot see my way to any
decent abridgement or modification. I have made up my
mind also to the omission of the other two. I only wish I
had some good substitutes.

Keble's defence of his words, and his position, was consistent
and able: his recommendation of the Ave and his reverence for
the Virgin Mother was based on Scriptural authority and the
doctrines of the Universal Church, as he explained, and had
nothing to do with what might have been interpreted publicly
as a leaning towards Roman Catholicism. At a crucial time of
difficulty, however, in the relationship between the Church of
England and the Church of Rome, when the Oxford Movement
was held responsible for Romanist tendencies which persuaded
people to alter their faith, and with Newman prominently in
mind, Coleridge and Dyson were anxious that Keble should not
expose himself to any more charges which might imply heresy.
'Mother out of Sight', it was feared might have led to the wrong
conclusions: the poem first bore the title, 'The Annunciation',
(St John XIX, 27). It was inspired by an incident which
occurred when the Kebles were in the Highlands in August
1844. Keble was visiting a Mr Stuart when the son of the house
came into the room looking for his mother: she was not there
and the boy exclaimed sorrowfully, 'My mother is not here'.
The boy's tone touched Keble and led him on to thoughts of
Christ and Mary, and the Church and Mary:

> What if our English air be stirr'd
> With sighs from saintly bosoms heard,

Or penitents to learning angels dear, —
'Our own, our only Mother is not here.'

And so Keble went on to argue and advise that due reverence should be paid to Christ's mother:

Thenceforth, whom thousand worlds adore,
He calls thee Mother evermore;
Angel nor Saint His face may see
Apart from what He took of thee;
How many we choose but name thy Name,
Echoing below their high acclaim
In Holy Creeds? since earthly song and prayer
Must keep faint time to the dread Anthems there.

How but in love on thine own days,
Thou blissful One, upon thee gaze?
Nay every day, each suppliant hour,
Whene'er we kneel, in aisle or bower,
Thy glories we may greet unblam'd,
Nor shun the lay by Seraphs framed.
Hail Mary full of grace! O welcome sweet,
Which daily in all lands all Saints repeat;

- - - -

Therefore, as kneeling day by day,
We to Our Father duteous pray;
So unforbidden we may speak,
An Ave to Christ's Mother meek.
(As children with 'good-morrow' come,
To Elders in some happy home,)
Inviting to the Saintly Host above,
With our unworthiness to pray in love.

Clearly Keble made the point that the Ave to Mary was not forbidden; but it was dangerous ground, and he gave way reluctantly to the advice of Dyson and Coleridge while not in any way changing his mind about the poem as his letter to Coleridge showed.

Keble's position remained firmly on the foundation of the original, universal Church, the Church of St Paul, of the Apostolic Succession and of the Early Fathers. He did not feel the irresistible pull of the Roman Church as Newman did: Newman's conclusion was that he had 'a strong intellectual conviction that the Roman Catholic System and Christianity were convertible terms'. This was not so with Keble: in the Church of Rome there lay beliefs to which he could never reconcile himself. He wrote to Coleridge in 1841:

> I cannot go to Rome till Rome be much changed indeed; but I may be driven out of the English Church, should that adopt the present set of Charges and Programmes; and many will, I fear, not be content to be nowhere, as I should feel it my duty to try to be.[7]

In the same letter Keble expressed his unhappiness that some of his brethren, of the first order in the clergy, were denying the Church of England's claim to be part of the Universal Church of Christ: they refused to acknowledge its catholicity. Again Keble emphasised his position:

> As to Rome, I thought I had said in my letter to you, that come what will, it would be impossible — [twice underscored] for me to join it until it is other than it is at present; Archbishop Laud's saying as I think; and I suppose you would not yourself say, that if Rome altered her terms of communion to a certain extent, such communion ought not to be sought. The contingency that I contemplate, a very dreary one, but such an one as I, ought not to think it strange if I incur it, is, not going to Rome, but being driven out of all communion whatever. I cannot hide it from myself that two Prelates have distinctly denied an Article of the Apostles' Creed, the H.C.Ch.; and that while no notice is taken of them, attempts are being being made in Oxford, and in many Dioceses at once, to enforce a view equivalent to theirs; which view if it were adopted, would drive me, and, as I suppose, all Catholic Christians, out of Communion.

The Holy Catholic Church was an essential article of belief in the Church of England: if this were not recognised, then Keble had no alternative than to cease communion.

The catholicity which the Roman Church claimed, however, was another matter. Certainly Keble understood that there was a close relationship between his Church and the Church of Rome; but he knew that Rome had erred. He saw no reason to accept the Pope's word as infallible and all-powerful over the words of his other bishops: he saw no authority, neither in the Scriptures, nor in the history of the Church, for this view: nor was it sanctioned by the Early Fathers. There were other wanderings away from the true path which Keble likewise condemned, and which he considered the Reformed Church of England had avoided; for example, the doctrine of transubstantiation was a snare and a delusion. Keble denied absolutely the gross, carnal Presence: Christians did not take part in some sanctified cannibalistic rite. He did not, however, deny the Real Presence in another more spiritual and inspired, rather than physical way, as his stalwart defences of both Peter Young and Archdeacon Denison showed.

On the other hand there was much in Roman Catholic practice, and in its ritual, which Keble could see was backed by the authority of history. In 1844 a controversy arose over a proposed translation of the Roman Catholic Breviary, and Keble wrote to Pusey saying that the Church of England should not be put off from using all that was of Catholic authority:

> With regard to the risk of publishing an English Breviary at all, even in the most expurgated shape, I own I cannot well comprehend it, that is, I cannot comprehend how it should have a Romeward tendency with good sort of persons; but to say that our Church cannot bear such a book, and that it is inconsistent with loyalty to her, this, it seems to me, would be a very scandalous sort of thing.[8]

It was yet another example of Keble standing his ground, refusing to be reticent, and not recognising that discretion was considered by many to be the better part of valour. Earlier, on 19 March 1842, when the Peter Young controversy was still smouldering on, Keble wrote to his brother Thomas:

By the bye, will Isaac [Williams] tell me what he means by saying that on account of someone's being inclined to Rome, he would wish me to do as little as possible just now? I thought the reason for publicity was to show people that they need not go to Rome on account of this doctrine at least.[9]

The argument over the doctrine of the Real Presence was, to Keble's mind, a valuable chance to demonstrate one of the errors of the Church of Rome, and the opportunity to mark publicly one of the distinctions between the Anglican communion and that of Rome. The trouble was that less able and less intelligent men than Keble did not appreciate the details of doctrine, and always viewed differences with the Church of Rome on a broader front; and to a certain extent Keble knew this but refused to grant it much importance. He wrote to Thomas on 30 November 1841,

... except that poor Golightly has done today the wildest of all his freaks: he has put a letter in *The Standard* with his name, announcing by name Ward, Bloxam, Mozley and others (at least I think there were others) as being really Papists. But the letter is almost incoherent.[10]

Keble's support lay in sound theological scholarship, in the writings of the Early Christian Fathers, and in the history of the Church: it was, perhaps, too much to ask popular opinion to judge the finer points of doctrine in the light of scholarship. Certainly Keble felt it his duty to do so. Newman's 'strong intellectual conviction' may, in the end, have made him choose Rome; but here was an equally strong, if not stronger, intellect that saw that Rome was not the true Church to speak for all Christianity. Contrary to what most of his friends thought, Keble considered that it was a time for the Church of England to speak out. It was true that some people were defecting to the Church of Rome. A.O.J. Cockshut in his book *Anglican Attitudes* gives a slightly false impression when he makes the general statement about the 1840s and 1850s, providing no statistics, that 'increasing numbers of educated people were joining the Roman Catholic Church or abandoning religion altogether'. It is equally true to say, in a general way, that many educated people were standing firm with the Church of England, defending its ancestry, and arguing its cause: foremost among them was John Keble.

Similarly, A.O.J. Cockshut misjudges Keble when writing about the Erastian Crisis and, in particular, about Manning, Hope and Robert Wilberforce who were all to join the Church of Rome. He writes:

> For Manning and Hope as for Newman, the Church of England deserved loyalty only so long as it could show how it fitted into the scheme of a universal Church. For Keble faith in the Church of England was primary, and the idea of a universal Church was something that had to be fitted into the Anglican system. For Keble the whole affair provided much grief but no uncertainty, and no intellectual difficulty at all.[11]

That the controversy with the Roman Church caused Keble much grief, there can be no doubt at all: his letters continually record it whether to his friends or to his brother. They also record his uncertainty. Sir John Coleridge wrote in his *Memoir*:

> There may be many, not perhaps those who have read or thought most deeply on the controversy, who can see in all this no reasonable, or even excusable grounds for doubt, or trouble of mind. Keble, however, was not one of those; he had both; and it is a matter for the deepest gratitude that he was supported under them, and guided safely through them.

Coleridge was right about Keble's troubled thoughts and he quoted from a letter which Keble had written in 1843:

> It may be that I do not see my way clearly in the controversy between us and Rome; but as long as I was in doubt, and perhaps a good deal longer than I might seem to myself in speculation to be so, I should think it my duty to stay where I am ... No private judgement of the comparative perfection of another Church, did such exist,

would at all justify such a change. This, as far as I understand myself, is my present judgement in this awful
matter; but, believe me, my dearest friend, I want prayer
and help quite as much as N., though for very different
reasons.[12]

He wrote, too in the same letter that in order to leave one
Church for another, the conviction had to be deliberate and
willing, accepted not only by the heart and conscience, but also
by the intellect. There can be no doubt that Keble's intellectual
difficulties were great and he continually resorted to the
traditional authorities of the Church in order to re-assess or
reassure himself in his position: he went to the seventeenth
century Divines and to the Early Church Fathers. There he
found the answers which helped him resolve his doubts and
problems: intellectually, it was his scholarship which convinced
him of the Church of England's claim to be the true inheritor of
the proper Universal Church. The crisis of the 1840s, in the end,
reinforced Keble's position as strong champion of the Church of
England.

Undoubtedly too, in some measure, Keble was the victim of
the receiving idea. The Church he had been brought up in had
attractions for him that it was difficult to resist, and his
conservative nature made him extremely loath to cast off old
allegiances. In the same letter to Coleridge Keble remarked:
'Few persons have a stronger feeling than I of the duty of
continuing where one's lot is cast; except where the call to go
elsewhere is very plain.' Neither emotionally, nor intellectually,
was that call plain in Keble's case.

Naturally his upbringing, his family background, helped to
form Keble's religious attitude. Walter Lock[13] wrote that 'the
traditions of the family were Cavalier and Nonjuring'. The Non-
jurors had refused to take the Oath of Allegiance to William III,
many because they refused to break the Oath which they had
already sworn to James II: they held a high view of the
dignity and authority of the King, even, when the King was a
Roman Catholic. The extremists among them, one of whom was
George Hickes (1642-1715) who had been Dean of Worcester,
thought that the Church of England had lost its claim to be
considered a true church: they held that the Non-jurors alone

could be considered the true, catholic and apostolic succession in England. Their predecessors, the Laudians of Commonwealth days, had not carried on episcopal succession among their own numbers. But the apostolic succession and the corporate authority of the bishops were issues which both Laudians and Non-jurors believed were vital to the integrity of their religious views. The same two issues were of vital importance for Keble too.

NOTES

1. E.F.L. Wood, 'John Keble', *Leaders of the Church 1800-1900*, London, 1909, p.53.
2. Wood, pp.53-4.
3. Wood, p.68.
4. Sir J.T. Coleridge, *A Memoir of the Rev. John Keble*, 3rd ed., Oxford, 1870. Vol. II, p.291.
5. Dyson was a close friend of Keble, who had been an undergraduate with him at Corpus Christi College, Oxford. See Coleridge, Vol. I, pp.35-46.
6. 'Mother of God.'
7. Coleridge, Vol. II, p.299.
8. Quoted by Wood, p.54.
9. Correspondence of John Keble, Keble College Library. The Keble family correspondence is arranged chronologically, sorted into numbered envelopes contained in boxes. The footnotes will show the Library's catalogue reference and the envelope number, as in this instance, C15.
10. Correspondence, C15.
11. A.O.J. Cockshut, *Anglican Attitudes*, London, 1959, p.44.
12. Coleridge, *Memoir*, Vol. II, p.301.
13. Walter Lock, *John Keble*, 7th ed., London, 1895, p.3.

CHAPTER 2

Vital Principles

1 *Tradition*

The vital principles of Keble's religious thought which underlie his poetry were, in large part, determined by his family background, and gradually confirmed, after many mental struggles, by his meticulous scholarship and intelligent judgement: they lay firmly at the basis of Keble's writings alike in prose and poetry. However, the high regard in which he held the Non-jurors, for example, was not shared by all his friends. Pusey wrote to Keble that he had thought the Stuarts were rightly dethroned until he had listened to Keble on the subject; and that on one occasion when he had made a deprecatory remark about the Non-jurors, Keble had replied, 'I cannot think that the Non-jurors' position was so very bad or useless an one. I seem to trace our present life in good measure to it.'[1]

It is interesting to note Keble's persuasiveness in argument. His earnestness, intensity and utter conviction, at the same time combined with an astounding quiet humility from all accounts, add a clear dimension to the character of this man so revered by many Anglicans and many others besides. Sir John Coleridge recorded that he preferred to express his oppositions to Keble, when they had disagreements, in correspondence rather than in conversation. He thought he could do so more freely, with fewer inhibitions, 'although I always felt not merely the superiority of his intellect, but of his knowledge on most of the subjects we discussed'.

Charles Dyson, too, found it difficult to combat Keble in conversation. Coleridge wrote:

But I remember conversing with Dyson on some matter, 'Synods' I believe, on which Keble and I had differed. He happened to agree with me, 'But then', said he, 'when Keble is with me discussing such things, he is so earnest, and I have such a feeling, that one with so much holiness, as well as learning and ability, must be right, that I

23

succumb at the time to arguments and assertions, which,
when I think them over afterwards, do not always satisfy
my reason, or my acquaintance with history.'[2]

However, while drawing attention to Keble's power in
conversation even other men of powerful intellect, and while he
used Dyson as an example, he did qualify the example in
particular by stating that Dyson did not adhere to the same
method of historical interpretation as Keble. Dyson thought
that in looking back into time, men should not be 'fettered by
the forms and precedents of antiquity, but should look to the
spirit and to the circumstances of respective ages', which was
hardly the method of a true scholar.

For Keble, in the prime matter of the Christian religion, it
was necessary to scrutinise the evidence. So his religious
thought tended always to rely on the authority of the
Scriptures, on the authority of the Early Christian Fathers, on
the authority of the bishops, the inheritors of the apostles, and
on the authority of the Church's history. Yet if his religious
position was close to that of the Church of Rome, there were
still many irreconcilable difficulties. The supreme position of
the Pope, and differences over the sacraments, were primary
obstacles which separated the Church of England from the
Church of Rome.

The Puritan position was untenable. To rest your faith on a
literal interpretation of the New Testament was obtuse and
absurd. Not even Bishop Andrewes's liberalism could have
been acceptable to Keble. Andrewes (1555-1626), a strong
defender of episcopacy as an integral part of the true Church,
had refused to unchurch those Christian bodies which had lost
their episcopate in the Reformation. He had said:

Even if our order be admitted to be of divine authority, it
does not follow that without it there can be no salvation, or
that without it a Church cannot stand. Only a blind man
could fail to see Churches standing without it. Only a man
of iron could deny that salvation is to be found within
them.[3]

Such 'a man of iron' was John Keble: in later days he was one who could not maintain such a latitude of judgement as Andrewes had held.

Certainly the Reformers did not enjoy Keble's greatest respect. When his sister Elizabeth was staying with Thomas in 1836, he enclosed a note for her in a letter to Thomas dated 14 November in which he wrote:

> As to the Reformers, I certainly do think that *as a set* they belonged to the same class with the Puritans and Radicals and I have very little doubt that if we had lived in those times, neither my Father nor you nor Prevost nor Harrison would have had anything to do with them. And I think we shall never be able to make our ground good against either Romanists or Puritans till we have separated ourselves and our liturgy from them.[4]

In the same way that Keble censured the Reformers, in his own time he was extremely critical of those men in the Church of England who, like Bishop Andrewes had been, were broad in outlook and latitudinarian in principle. Thomas Arnold, who had joined Keble at Corpus Cristi College in 1811, proved a great disappointment. Keble's letters in Keble College Library trace the regret, the censure, the separation and the final *rapprochement*, concerning the way in which Arnold thought about the Church. To start with, Arnold and Keble had been great friends. In a letter to Thomas Keble, dated 22 December 1827, Keble wrote indicating that he had acted as a referee for Thomas Arnold. 'What do you think of Tom Arnold's success at Rugby? Don't you think I must have writ a capital letter for him?'[5] And in 1828 the relationship had not changed: again Keble wrote to his brother on 29 March:

> I staid in Oxford till yesterday afternoon to see Tom Arnold, who came up to dispute himself into a B.D. He seems just the same as when I saw him, both in body and mind.[6]

Yet serious differences of opinion were soon to become apparent. In 1834 Keble wrote to his brother, 'Here is the 2nd tom. of tom Arnold, more dismaying to me than anything that has gone before.' The light-heartedness which can be detected in the tone of this letter was to disappear completely when Thomas Arnold considered Keble's opposition, with others in Oxford, to Dr Hampden's proposed appointment as Regius Professor to be no more than 'lynch law'. In April 1836 Arnold published an attack on the Tractarians in the *Edinburgh Review* under the title of 'The Oxford Malignants', a title for which the editor was responsible but to which Arnold agreed. The breach between Keble and Arnold came.

Firm principles were involved, and yet this division caused Keble great regret. In a letter to Thomas Keble uncertainly marked as 1838 but which according to Sir John Coleridge's summary could have been written as late as 1840, Keble recorded:

> I have received this morning a very kind letter from Thos. of Rugby, in so mitigated and so friendly a tone as bids fair to open up again the communication between us. He says, when he wrote that affair in the *Edinburgh Review*, he did not know that I had anything to do with the anti-Hampden proceedings which made him so angry. Altogether I am in good hope he is beginning to think better of things tho of course one cannot be sanguine as to his coming right round.[7]

Late in 1840 Keble had written to George Cornish: 'His [Tom Arnold's] feelings seem much mitigated towards his old friends; but I wish I could see some fair sign of his taking a better view of great questions.'[8]

Although it is inconceivable that Arnold did not realise that Keble was closely associated with those who campaigned against Hampden,[9] Keble was pleased to accept the offer of reconciliation on the level of personal friendship: he was never to accept, however, that Arnold was right in principle. On 31 December 1840 Keble wrote to his brother:

> I have heard from G. Cornish today, and he mentions Arnold, and talks of the pain he suffers from old friends separating from him and from being attacked, as he says, in error, — so much that I feel a little qualmish about the

leaf of the Mysticism which I here inclose to you. I want
you to put yourself in his place and see whether I have said
what he may reasonably complain of ... G.C. ... seems to
have enjoyed his visit to Rugby, and I gather from what he
says that T.A. is rather mollified: they say Bunsen does
him much good but I am afraid it is but in a Conservative
sort of way.[10]

So the old personal wounds were healed: Keble and Arnold,
despite the former's 'Newmanism', to use Arnold's own term,
and despite the latter's latitudinarianism, resumed their
friendship. Keble took a kindly and close interest in his
godson Matthew's career, and on Advent Sunday in 1840, he
drew his brother, Thomas's attention to Matthew's Oxford
achievement: the letter is additionally interesting because it
records part of the history of the preparation for Keble's Tract
89, 'On the Mysticism attributed to the Early Fathers of the
Church':

> You will see that Matthew Arnold is Scholar of Balliol
> after a very hard contest. I sent him a little book with a
> note which I hope will not do any harm. I did not see him ...
> I left the 5 first portions on Mysticism with N for
> publication as a Tract and now I am going to work with the
> Translation of S. Gregory Naz. as fast as I can — I mean,
> with Wilson's Translation of it.
>   There are lots of new books coming out. Bowden's
> Gregory, Newman's Vth lot of Sermons, some more of St.
> Chrys., a work of Gladstone's etc. etc.[11]

Nevertheless, Thomas Arnold's interpretation of what the
principles of the Church of England should be, deeply saddened
Keble. He grieved, at Thomas Arnold's death and afterwards,
about Arnold's serious errors. He lamented to his brother in a
letter dated 6 June 1844:

> It is a real refreshment to write to you after looking over a
> good deal of poor dear Tom Arnold's Remains, which book,
> if I had not grown far harder and more unfeeling than I
> could wish, would distress me, I really think, more than

anything that had been published for years, and that in a
great variety of ways.[12]

The passage of time had worked on both Keble and Arnold:
poor Arnold was a cause for tears to be shed rather than for
anathematization. Keble attributed his resignation about
Arnold's writings to his hardness as a result of experience, but
perhaps Keble too, as he had said of Arnold, had rather been
mollified by the process of time.

So the clash with Arnold had been one of Church principles;
and it was a typical stand, of the many which Keble took during
his life, against the broad interpretation of doctrine and against
unsound ideas about the nature of the Church of England. It
was the influence of Keble's origin, his background and his
upbringing, and his being nurtured in the ideas of his father,
that moulded his religious thought; and it was his own intellect
which later investigated the validity of his beliefs and
confirmed him in them.

Not so was Newman's development. His life was a steady
progress in a change of ideas from Evangelicalism to Roman
Catholicism. Keble's religious thought needed only to be
confirmed: he found this confirmation, in the seventeenth
century Divines, in people such as Nicholas Ferrar, who found
consolation in a life of retirement and who founded a retreat
which became known as the 'Arminian Monastery'; in George
Herbert, the country parish priest who stands out in the history
of English literature as the poet *par excellence* of Anglicanism;
and in Richard Hooker, as well as in the Early Fathers, many of
whose ideas he found so compatible with his own.

Herbert's poems quite clearly held inspiration and example of
pattern for some of Keble's own poetry: many thoughts and
themes are similar, and a comparison has been made between
The Temple and *The Christian Year*.[13] Yet perhaps even more
important in the understanding of Keble's mind is the example
which Herbert's prose work *A Priest to the Temple, or The
Country Parson* would have given him. Certainly the work was
one which Keble read and contemplated: it is contained,
together with Herbert's poems, and the life of Herbert by Isaac
Walton, in the shelves of Keble's personal library preserved in
the stacks of Keble College Library. It is impossible to miss

the great similarity between Keble's way of life, or rather the way in which he tried to lead his life, and the advice and rules which Herbert laid down for the country parson. In many instances it is as though Herbert's writing is a description of John Keble: 'The Countrey Parson is full of all knowledg', or, 'The Countrey Parson hath read the Fathers also, and the schoolmen, and the later Writers, or a good proportion of all', or again, 'The Countrey Parson preacheth constantly, the pulpit is his joy and throne: if he at any time intermit, it is either for want of health, or against some great Festivall, that he may the better celebrate it, or for the variety of the hearers, that he may be heard at his returne more attentively.' The rules and precepts which Herbert formulated must have represented for Keble an ideal way of life, not always possible to follow, which Keble undoubtedly tried to imitate. He turned his back on an attractive, academic career at Oxford, and shunned the public light except for those times when he considered it absolutely necessary to speak out. Otherwise, he tried to lead a conscientious life as a proper parish priest, the shepherd of his flock, rejoicing when he married young people who were not constrained to do so because the girl was pregnant, and encouraging the practice of Confession because he held that it helped him to know the real state of mind of his parishioners. Such an example he found in George Herbert, and it was one which he felt other priests in the Church of England would have done well to follow.

As with Herbert, so with Keble (though in a much more scholarly way), the basic tenets of the Church of England underlie all his writing both prose and poetry, and all his preaching; and a definition of those tenets should be made. After the Reformation, the Church of England maintained what it held to be the Universal Catholic faith in Christ set forth in the Scriptures, the Creeds and in the decisions of the first four General Councils; it upheld what it considered to be the Catholic precept of the supremacy of the Scriptures in matters of doctrine and conduct; it upheld the provision of worship in a language understood by the people; it encouraged bible-reading by the laity; it upheld the giving of the Communion to the laity in both kinds, both the bread and the wine; and it maintained the laying on of hands by the bishop as an essential rite in

Confirmation and Ordination. The Church encouraged regular Communion by all the faithful, maintaining the three orders of the ministry, bishops, priests, and deacons, kept the succession of the bishops from the Apostles, kept the liturgical order of the Christian year, and it did not recognise the supremacy of the Pope as that had developed since the days of Gregory VII. It denied the Pope's authority to interfere in the secular affairs of any state and his power to depose princes, recognised liberty for national Churches in the fellowship of Christ's Holy Catholic Church 'to decree Rites or Ceremonies' (Article XX), rejected scholastic philosophy and late medieval definitions based on it such as transubstantiation, rejected the ideas of purgatory, indulgences and the merits of the saints all of which had been abused in the late medieval period, retained the medieval ideas of property, jurisdiction and of ecclesiastical administration, maintained a continuity of administration which extended throughout the time of the Reformation's troubles onwards, and it claimed to be a living, important part of the worldwide Church of Christ.

All these tenets of the Church of England were implicit in Keble's religious thought: he held in the greatest respect the liturgy of the Book of Common Prayer together with the XXXIX Articles of Faith. Keble was always assiduous to guard and uphold the Articles. Those which, through controversy and dissent, proved open to interpretation, he was at great pains to render correctly with the help of all the authority of the Scriptures, the Fathers, and the bishops in the history of the Church, which his intellect and scholarship could deduce.[14]

A first example of his writing which shows clearly his underlying principles, and which became a companion piece to the Prayer Book for many in the nineteenth century, was *The Christian Year*. It was first published in 1827, anonymously, when Keble was thirty-five, and comprised a volume of poems which were suited to the important days in the Christian year. It was a book of devotion, a sort of complement to the Prayer Book, which he published, in the end, reluctantly because he felt many of the poems to be personal and intimate. John Davison in particular, one of his old Oriel College circle of friends, persuaded Keble to publish. Keble wrote to Davison:

I have got a few attempts at hymns by me, which I have from time to time written, principally for my own relief in the many hours I spend ... My plan was to have one, if I could, for every Sunday and holiday in the year: taking the hint for the subject of each from something or other in the proper Psalms or Lessons of the day ... but so many copies have been allowed to be taken, principally by friends of my sisters, that it seems already in some degree broken in upon: and one has been printed in a collection by Mr J. Marriott, without my knowledge.[15]

He went on to ask Davison for his criticisms of the hymns he had enclosed. Later, on 28 May 1825, Keble wrote to Davison and remarked: 'So upon the whole I think I have made up my mind to follow your advice and that of some others of my friends, and print at least a selection, in the most useful and plainest way that I can.'[16]

Keble's friends thought the poems too good, and too morally valuable to leave hidden. The famous facts of *The Christian Year's* success (see p.112), ninety-five editions in the space of the author's lifetime, proved their point.[17]

In 1876 Dr Barry in Lecture IV of a series entitled 'Companions of the Devout Life' showed how the quietness of the poetry's tone, and its constant sense of the presence of God in Nature, in Humanity and in the Church, fitted *The Christian Year* to be a proper companion of the devout life. The poems dealt with, and alluded to, the Old Testament, the New Testament, the Apocrypha, the Fathers, the Prayer Book, the ideas of Bishop Butler, and the poetic ideas of Spenser, Herbert, Milton, Waller, Gray and Wordsworth, to mention a few whose notes ring through Keble's poems.

Keble hoped that the poems would make people think about God much more in their daily life. Certainly *The Christian Year* became a family book, and from reading it people must have derived some feeling of comfort and consolation. Perhaps there was created in them some sentimental glow of affection for the Church and all the qualities and virtues it stood for. In addition, Keble managed to reconcile people to their lot:

> If on our daily course of mind
> Be set to hallow all we find,
> New treasures still, of countless price,
> God will provide for sacrifice.

- - - -

> The trivial round, the common task,
> Would furnish all we ought to ask;
> Room to deny ourselves, a road
> To bring us, daily, nearer God.
> — 'Morning.'

and in the poem for the Sixteenth Sunday after Trinity:

> The wanderer seeks his native bower,
> And we will look and long for Thee,
> And thank Thee for each trying hour,
> Wishing, not struggling, to be free.

In this Keble succeeded: such poems became favourite hymns. And from the everyday, domestic scene, Keble led his readers to think more deeply than usual on matters of faith, and principles of the Church. It was obvious that the ideas which lay behind many of the poems were bred by Keble's early life and education, and they were enlarged on, developed and further explained in what he wrote and preached later.

It is noticeable that Keble's style of address and tone altered to suit the audience he expected to have. Most of the sermons collected in *Sermons Occasional and Parochial* (Oxford, 1868) were intended for the ordinary church congregation and their tone tends to be didactic and explicit. Nevertheless, they show the important themes in his religious thought, to many of which he was often to return. Sermon IX was preached at Eastleach on 15 June 1817 after a terrible winter following bad harvests when the price of wheat rose, by the end of 1816, from fifty-two shillings to upwards of one hundred shillings a quarter. It was from such events of real importance to the livelihood and well-being of ordinary people, that Keble was often able to draw lessons and examples for the instruction of his parishioners;

and, at the same time, it gives the lie to historians such as E.L. Woodward and novelists such as Thomas Hardy who create a false impression about the isolation of the Oxford Movement's leaders from the problems of the real world. Woodward wrote:

> The leaders of this movement for the restoration of authority were comparatively young men; in 1833 Newman was thirty-two, Froude thirty, Pusey thirty-three, and Keble forty-one. They knew little of the world to which their teaching was addressed, and there was an air of unreality about their hints at martyrdom while they were defending privilege, and about the 'emergency' which they alone had discovered.[18]

While in *Jude the Obscure* Hardy made it seem that the Movement's leaders were cut off from ordinary people, holy but enclosed within their stone walls, set apart from 'the grind of stern reality'.[19]

Keble's sermons and, moreover, his letters show this to be wrong. Keble knew only too well the troubles of the world, the problems of poverty, the difficulties of domestic economy and the ravages of disease. From Fairford, on 29 March 1828, he wrote to his brother that 'The Typhus is very rife in 4 families all in a bunch at the top of the town'; and in 1833 he mentioned the cholera epidemic at Bisley, 'Do you want money for your Cholera Fund? I empower you to draw on me for not less than £5 ...'[20] Elsewhere in his letters he comments on farm labourers breaking machines, mentions the condition of workhouses, shows his attitude to beer-houses and their effects on the population, and passes judgement on the price of corn and the distribution of allotments.[21]

In the present case of the steep rise in the price of wheat and the occasion of Sermon IX, Keble preached on the text 'A fruitful land maketh He barren, for the wickedness of them that dwell therein' (Psalm CVII, 34), and he showed how the wicked must expect punishment. Maintaining the principle that the Old Testament contained lessons applicable to the modern world, Keble drew example from, and analogy to, the stories of the Old Testament. He quoted the destruction of Sodom and Gomorrah, and the blasting of the soil of the Holy Land, which transformed it from the promised land flowing with milk and honey to the one described in Moses' frightening prophecy. He quoted the prophet Haggai in describing the plight which befell the children of Israel just returned from the captivity, 'Ye eat but ye have not enough ... Thus saith the Lord of Hosts, Consider your ways.' He referred to another prophet, Joel, who spoke of a serious famine which happened to the impenitent Jews, and compared it with the harvests of 1816 in many parts of England. Keble attributed the evils of his time to the wickedness of England's people. He pointed out to his congregation that St Paul had given good warning 'Be not deceived; neither fornicators, nor idolators, nor adulterers, nor effeminate ... shall inherit the Kingdom of God.' He made it quite clear that the wicked had to repent in order to achieve salvation:

I say then, my brethren, that the blood of those many souls who are perishing for ever through uncleanness in this land of ours, must needs cling to its soil, and cry aloud to heaven for vengeance upon it; and vengeance will come, doubt it not, it will come sooner or later, and will not spare, if it be not stayed by a mighty sorrow, a true humiliation, an effectual amendment.

He particularised the faults:

Pride, covetousness, extravagance, drunkenness, unclean-ness, maliciousness, for which, if we would escape the arrows of God's wrath now and hereafter, we are bound to humble ourselves day and night before Him, in our own behalf and in the behalf of this whole nation; these are the accursed things which must in any wise be put away out of the camp of Israel.[22]

In such a way Keble sought to show his rural parishioners what he himself firmly believed, that the Old Testament stories had relevance for their life with all its predicaments. Not that he afforded them any immediate comfort: the remedy for their situation lay in the supposed goodness of their future conduct. Admonitions from the pulpit baked and buttered no bread for the starving poor. Nevertheless, he was careful to show the principle of Article VII, that 'The Old Testament is not contrary to the New'. He emphasised the New as the inevitable and necessary complement to the Old; and from the Old he took his examples, and pointed many a moral parallel.

In looking back to the Old Testament, it can be seen that Keble was a careful and conservative thinker who did not easily discard what was old in favour of the revolutionary new, and as he was a conservative in Anglican theology, so too he was conservative in politics. Such was his temperament, and, no doubt, his upbringing cast the mould. Certainly his political sympathies lay with the Tories rather than with the Whigs: his correspondence shows this fact. Self-confessedly, he wrote to his brother's family in 1834:

> My Dears,
> 'When grass grows in Janiveer,
> 'twill grow the worse for it all the year.'
> So says Mr Fuller in the Book of Proverbs that I so kindly gave to G.C. and wish now I had them at hand: for they are very useful to us Tory scribblers.[23]

Later, in the same year, although the day is not signified, he wrote to Thomas:

> We **are** going to get rid of all our Coln Beer-houses, in regard to which Squire Beach uttered a sentiment today which struck me as genuine True Blue — I said 'we must make up our mind to lose a vote or two', and he said 'O never mind the votes as long as we are doing right.'[24]

In another letter of that year Keble wrote down a piece of doggerel verse which showed his own implicit faith in his conservative cast of mind:

> Why do you cry, 'Blue for ever' I pray?
> Sir, you know better than I can say:
> But if you must know, I've been told in my youth
> That Blue is the tint of unchanging *Truth*:
> And when I look up to the sky so bright,

It really would seem that the lesson was right,
But none, when I look at the noble shew
Of the blue-ribband-wearers wherever I go.

Earlier in the year he had passed a remark that women on Sundays were wearing unobtrusively bits of blue showing their political allegiance. In this letter he added: 'Mr Barber's harvest-home waggon was conducted home by a boy on the forehorse quite covered with blue ribbands or ribbons. What do you think of that?'[25]

It is clear from the correspondence that in Keble's mind there was some connection between right thinking in religious matters and a proper attitude in politics. There is a note of amused disgust in a letter to Thomas dated 20 February 1840: 'Mr Ch. Bailey, my Churchwarden has just been signing Lord Ashley's paper about Schools, heartily, as he told me, because he believes the Church Established is a *Liberal Church*.'[26] Keble's emphasis made his feeling obvious. And on Ash Wednesday 1840, he wrote again to Thomas: 'I am quite relieved at seeing in the Paper today that the Bps have agreed on a Ch. Discipline Bill which satisfies my Lord of [Exon]. They say the socialists are fast going downhill in this neighbourhood.'[27]

However, conservative as he was by nature, and although he regarded novelty with distrust, his religious thought did show development throughout his lifetime. At certain periods, often because of political situations which he believed were about to affect the Church to its detriment. Keble found himself forced by conscience to state his religious position firmly and forcefully. The Reform Act of 1832, and subsequently the suppression by the Government of ten Irish sees, constituted the most important political action which prompted Keble to give his famous Assize Sermon of 1833 which Newman marked as the beginning of the Oxford Movement.

2 *Tracts, Treatises and Sermons*

As a conservative in religious thinking Keble found his greatest guard against any liberal, wayward temptations, in the watch-words 'Don't be original', which, no doubt, Keble had learned from his study of Greek literature where the principle of plagiarism was not frowned upon, Newman recalled: 'I recollect his borrowing a friend's sermon, which had been preached before the University, and, I suppose, had been well spoken of to him. When he returned it, he whispered into his friend's ear, "Don't be original."'[28] Undoubtedly, this was his own reason for continually relying on the examples which guided Christian conduct and which were to be found in the Old Testament. His recognition of the phrase's sentiment is obvious in his poetry as shown later in his adherence to traditional forms, to Miltonic and Biblical imagery. Certainly, in all his writing and preaching he practised restraint which he unreservedly recommended to others.

It did not mean, however, that Keble lacked determination, or a considerable degree of rhetorical aggresiveness, when he felt the time demanded an unflinching stand on religious principle. Such was the case when he felt his Church being attacked by the infidel. The Hanoverian period had seen the Convocations silenced, the Church in a state of apathy and torpor, daily services stopped, and many holy days unobserved. Then with the Repeal of the Test Act, the Act of Catholic Emancipation and the Reform Act of 1832, followed by the promise of the Act suppressing the ten Irish sees, Keble saw the autonomy and authority of the episcopate being undermined. At variance with Arnold, who thought that the faults, especially in administration and finance, lay within the Church itself, Keble decided that 'scoundrels must be called scoundrels'. The poems of *Lyra Apostolica* struck the note of defiance:

> ... against the ruffian band,
> Come to reform where ne'er they came to pray.

Keble took the opportunity of warning the country against interfering with the sacred responsibilities of bishops in the Church by preaching the sermon on National Apostasy before Her Majesty's Judges of Assize from St Mary's pulpit, Oxford, on 14 July 1833.

In it he warned the nation about neglecting their responsibilities to the principles of religion embodied in the

Church of England, and admonished the many who had turned away from God altogether. He reminded people that the Old Testament revealed God's providence towards Christian nations and towards Christian individuals. The Old Testament stories stood as a series of analogies from which people might learn. He reproached parents for committing 'their children to be educated' and encouraged them to intermarry 'in houses, on which Apostolical Authority would rather teach them to set a mark as unfit to be entered by a faithful servant of Christ'.

There was little doubt, Keble thought, that people were indulging or encouraging a profane dislike of God's Awful Presence: there was a general tendency to leave Him out of all their thoughts.

Previously, of course, Keble had hoped that *The Christian Year* would help people to think more and more on the presence of God in their daily lives. It was a pious hope, and, as its publication figures show, there was some justification in thinking that it had succeeded. But its reading was not to everyone's taste, and not everyone knew about it, or cared to know about it. Keble recognised the ranks of the infidel swelling and their influence waxing.

He went on in the sermon to complain 'that the disrespect to the Successors of the Apostles, as such, is an unquestionable symptom of enmity to Him, who gave them their commission at first, and has pledged Himself to be with them for ever'. He drew the analogy of Saul who persecuted David his divinely ordained successor. It was to be realised, Keble warned, that the nation which infringes on Apostolical rights, will end in persecuting the Church itself. Too often the excuse of state security was given, as when Saul sought the life of David.

If apostacy was to be the case in England (Keble was implying that Apostacy would certainly exist if the Irish sees were suppressed, which, of course, they were), like Samuel, the devout should hold fast their ground and resolutely soldier on. Keble advised that the faithful should act as Samuel had done, and quoted the Scriptures: 'God forbid that I should sin against the Lord in ceasing to pray for you: but I will teach you the good and right way.' The Church, the laity and the clergy in their three orders of bishops, priests and deacons, should take to heart the Psalmist's inspiration: 'Fret not thyself because of the ungodly, neither be thou envious of the evil-doers: for they shall soon be cut down like the grass, and be withered even as the green herb.'

He advised intercession and remonstrance, calm, distinct and persevering, against any possible apostacy represented by any attack on the independence, integrity or autonomy of the bishops. He made it clear:

> To uphold and restore our endangered Church, will be for each of her anxious children to resign himself more thoroughly to his God and Saviour in duties public and private — daily and hourly duties, I mean, of piety, purity, charity and justice.

And finally Keble pointed out that people who were loyal to the Apostolical Church in England might have to wait long 'and very likely pass out of the world' before they could see any abatement 'in the triumph of disorder and irreligion'.

In Keble's mind, national apostasy did take place and Parliament suppressed the ten Irish sees. He decided to publish the sermon: a letter to Thomas shows that he thought carefully about its publication and sought advice. The letter was written in 1833, and although the day is not marked, it was obviously composed before 22 July 1833 when the sermon appeared:

> I have a month's mind to print and publish my Assize Sermon forthwith. If you don't write about it in 2 days time, I shall conclude you say yes to this. Palmer seemed to like it, which makes me hope it might answer.[29]

In the same letter, he went on to mention the Whigs' proposed bill to set up a body of commissioners to manage Church affairs, investigate endowments, forbid non-residence, create new sees and distribute the incomes of the richest bishoprics so that the poor parishes might gain greatly needed financial relief. Keble's opposition to the State's interference in Church matters was as obvious as it was predictable: 'It seems understood that the Abp. is going to take the high ground about the Erastian Bill; and that it is sure to be rejected.'

As well as privately, the warning against Erastianism was

made publicly in the printing of the Assize Sermon. Keble wrote in the Advertisement of the first edition that:

> The Legislature of England and Ireland (the members of which are not even bound to profess belief in the Atonement), this body has virtually usurped the commission of those whom our Saviour entrusted with at least one voice in making ecclesiastical laws, on matters wholly or partly spiritual.

He regarded the publication of the sermon as the least that could be done:

> ... unless we would have our children's children say, 'There was once here a glorious Church, but it was betrayed into the hands of libertines for the real or affected love of a little temporary peace and good order.

In this way, in the sermon, Keble had defined in sure terms two basic principles in his religious thought: the Apostolic Succession and the supreme authority of the bishops. Later, in 1834, he was one of the signatories in an Address to the Archbishop of Canterbury assuring His Grace of the signatories' sympathy and of their adherence to 'the Apostolic doctrine and polity of the Church'.

There can be no doubt that Keble thought the Church of England to be in great danger from possible interference from secular men in a secular parliament. At one stage in 1834 he wrote to his brother in a state of disillusionment that 'I propose founding a University in Sweden as the safest place, and having the Church in it'.[30]

However, a little earlier in 1833 the idea which was the germ of the Tracts had been mooted. Sir John Coleridge has recorded letters lobbying Dyson and Richards, an old friend of Keble's father, for support in the proposal 'to circulate right notions on the Apostolical Succession, and also for the defence of the Prayer Book against any sort of profane innovation'.[31] And on 16 August 1833 Keble wrote to his brother:

> ... and first of all we [illegible] you to know that Messrs

Palmer, Newman, Froude, and Keble have constituted
themselves into a Committee, to write round to their
friends and cronies, and know whether they would like to
be members of an (anonymous and secret) association for
diffusing right principles regarding the Apostolical
commission of the Clergy and protecting the Prayer book
from all profane innovation. If this be encouraged, it is
proposed for the first thing of all to get up and publish, as
cheap as possible, an account of St Ignatius, with extracts
from his works, and to follow it up from time to time with
other things in the same strain. Also if we can manage it,
to provide something more learned and ingenious for the
Clergy and educated people, to use them [sic] gradually to
primitive notions, and prepare them for what is very likely
to happen? I have only written two letters on it yet, one to
Ogilvie and one to Davison — both whose answers as well
yours, I shall look for with great anxiety.[32]

Undoubtedly, Keble was eager and busy with his letter writing,
considering the direct evidence of his writing to Dyson and
Richards as well as to Ogilvie and Davison: many other friends
must have been canvassed as well. It is interesting to note that,
in the same letter, Keble disclaims the Tractarians as
constituting a Party, the word '... as people use it, is a very
invidious term'. Nor is it generally realised that Keble very
nearly became editor of the Tracts: in 1835 he wrote to Thomas:
'Newman sends me word I am to be Editor of the Tracts. If so
one of the first must be 'Doctrines preacht by Mr T.K. and
excepted against by Mr J.K. the 4th Oct., 1835.'[33]

It was not to be the case; but Keble took up the theme of the
Assize Sermon in his contributions to the *Tracts for the Times*
(1833-41). In all, he composed eight, and the keynote of the first
seven was given in the title of No. 4, 'Adherence to the
Apostolical Succession, the Safest Course'. The clergy were
urged to take a higher view of their privilege as Christ's
ordained ministers. Keble stated that even if the doctrine was
not absolutely certain, then at least it was probable; and he
showed that there were sufficient indications in the New
Testament that it was Christ's will. The next six dealt with the

lectionary, the importance of Holy Baptism, the duty of Churchmen to avoid marriage with Dissenters: he returned to the subject of the Apostolic Ministry, expounded the history of the Doctrine, and emphasised that the Roman Church had minimised the Doctrine of Apostolical Succession in order to exalt the Papacy; and finally, he argued by historical instances that personal devotion was insufficient for the Christian Life, and Christians should take God's will exactly as it is declared in His Word, as interpreted by the Church.

Tract 89 (1840) was the most important in showing a basic principle of Keble's religious thought, and in Dean Church's view it was 'the most inopportune Tract' for it placed yet another weapon in the hands of the opposition. It was entitled 'Mysticism attributed to the Early Church Fathers' and although it was only half finished, it showed Pusey's influence in coverting the Tracts into Treatises.

Later, it will be shown how Keble's poetry exhibited many of the qualities, especially of symbolism and reserve, which Keble so much admired in the teachings of the Early Church Fathers, and which were discussed in Tract 89. In the Tract, Keble proposed to deal with four points concerning the vague charge of mysticism which had been used to discredit the Fathers. These were their figurative interpretation of the Scriptures, their fanciful application of Nature to spiritual realities, their readiness to see that Providence had interfered in the events of history, and their counsels of perfection which favoured a monastic and contemplative life. Yet in Tract 89 Keble dealt only with the first two points. He showed that the Fathers always upheld the doctrine of a permanent standard of morality yet they were far more lenient in judgement on the saints of the Old Testament than modern writers were. He attributed this to the fact that they apprehended God's presence in all things, and that they believed God's words and deeds were mystical in that they meant more than any human being was able to appreciate. Also, the Fathers felt a real bond with the Old Testament saints and their natural piety made them unwilling to condemn. The whole Jewish nation was to the Fathers 'a great prophet because He is great who was the subject of their prophecy'.[34]

Similarly with the New Testament, the words and actions of Christ, since they were the words and actions of God 'must mean far more than meets the eye or ear, they cannot but be full charged with heavenly and mysterious meaning'.

In considering Nature, Keble explained that the Fathers were not content with a mere scientific study of it, but that they were always piercing through to a mystical sense, which was analogous to the poet's use of illustrations from Nature. Keble considered Nature the poetry of God, 'a set of holy and divine associations and meanings wherewith it is His will to invest material things'. He recognised the truth of St Augustine's words, 'All beauty in Thy creatures is but so many beckonings of Thine.'[35]

The Tract stood as an uncompromising attack on the tendencies of contemporary, modern theology in Keble's time, and it was a magnificent specimen of the true reverence which Keble believed should be given to the Bible.

At this point, in thinking about the nature of God's revelation in different ways, it is appropriate to show the influence of Bishop Butler on Keble's religious thought. Butler, in his *Analogy*, accepted *a priori* arguments for theism, and he assumed the immortality of the soul. He adopted analogical reasoning as a system of looking for in Gladstone's words, 'a resemblance of qualitative relations'.[36] Butler thought that analogies could not be exact or perfect: it was sufficient if they were marked and substantive in many respects. Man did not deserve certainty on earth: probability was the highest form of knowledge attainable by man after the Fall. He argued that as the frame of man reveals a supreme conscience, so the frame of Nature shows a moral governor revealed through man's conscience. As this interpretation was involved with the acceptance of probability, Keble found in it a sort of philosophical confirmation of the theological principle of economy and reserve which he had learned from the Fathers. Keble regarded Butler as 'one of the safest teachers of religion, both natural and revealed, that ever blessed this Church'. He thought of him as the outstanding Anglican Divine who had watched over and carried on the Catholic traditions in the eighteenth century, and the *Analogy* was to him 'altogether a practical work, which aimed not at satisfying the mind, but at forming the heart and guiding the conduct, though the mind should remain unsatisfied'.[37] Butler's influence, in particular relationship to Keble's poetry, is further discussed in Part III.

Finding, in sympathy with Butler, support for the Church's true beliefs in the writings of the Early Fathers, Keble similarly accepted with Isaac Williams, the author of Tract 87 (1840) the doctrine of Reserve. Williams entitled his Tract 'Reserve in communicating Religious Knowledge'. Keble felt that religious knowledge and its expression, especially through poetry which he regarded as God's special means of religious communication, should be made with reserve, so that it could be gently grasped by the minds of those who had suited themselves for its reception. The true knowledge of the Church was not for the vulgar, not for the philistines, but rather for the initiated and instructed, for those who were prepared to ponder and meditate on images and symbols, and who would gradually see through the mysteries into the heart of Christian belief. Reserve was an esoteric theory, which Keble appreciated in the religious philosophy of the Fathers, and he reflected in his own poetry, for example, in the poem for the Fourth Sunday in Lent, *The Christian Year,* of which the last two stanzas run:

> He could not trust his melting soul
>   But in his Maker's sight—
> Then why should gentle hearts and true
> Bare to the rude world's withering view
>   Their treasure of delight!
>
> No — let the dainty rose awhile
>   Her bashful fragrance hide —
> Rend not her silken veil too soon,
> But leave her, in her own soft noon,
>   To flourish and abide.

This poem, written with two texts from Genesis in mind, one concerning Joseph privately weeping, and the other concerning Joseph making himself known to his brothers in private, embodied Keble's belief in Reserve. He drew the analogy with Nature who hides her beauty behind a veil which must be penetrated before the beauty can be appreciated. Similarly, we must wait for the rose to reveal the fullness of its beauty upon its final opening. So the true nature of the love of God, and the true nature of Christianity, is slowly revealed to those who are sufficiently interested to look for it. The beauty of the great truths, Keble thought, should not be 'soil'd by ruder breath', nor should it have to shrink from sight, 'Here in the coarse rude earth.' Again, other points about this poem, discussed in Part III, emphasise the relationship of the doctrine of Reserve to Keble's poetry.

Keble believed, with Isaac Williams, that sacred matters had to be handled with great reverence and respect, and the over-familiar treatment would bring them into contempt. It was on these grounds that Keble criticised Sir Walter Scott whom otherwise he very much admired:

> Situated as Scott was, we may and must regret, but we cannot severely censure, that inadequate sense of the religion of holy places, and of the appointed means of grace and Catholic communion, which permitted him, not occasionally, but as part of his settled plan of life, to substitute, during great part of the year, his own reading in his dining-room for the regular offices of the Church: we can allow for the unfavourable notion which he seems in general to have entertained of the Anglican clergy; of which class, as far as we recollect, he has not produced a single good specimen in all his novels from 'Kenilworth' to the 'Antiquary'.[38]

He went on to complain about Scott taking liberties with the words of Holy Scripture. He took exception

> ... to the irreverent introduction of Scripture phrases in familiar talk and corespondence, which, it is too plain from Scott's letters, and still more from some of those addressed to him, was practised among them as a matter of course. Painful as such expressions are, they are almost sure to be adopted, more or less unconsciously, even by persons who have no irreverent meaning, in a country where it is a part of religion to talk much of holy things, and to be fluent in quoting the most sacred words. It is, in short, the extreme Protestant rule of dispensing with all reserve about the Scriptures — such reserve as was religiously practised in

the ancient Church — to which we attribute in great
measure this grievous blot in a style otherwise so
delightful.[39]

Scott, then, was guilty of a lack of economy and reserve in
religious matters concerned particularly with the Scriptures,
and Keble's reproach about it in the review of Lockhart's *Life of
Sir Walter Scott*, published in the *British Critic* in 1838
underlined this fundamental principle of Keble's religious
thought.

Elsewhere, too, Keble treated the doctrine of Reserve. In
Tract 89, he had written of Origen, one of the Early Fathers:

> ... that it was by no means his custom, to trust his ordinary
> hearers with all the mysterious wonders, which he seemed
> to himself faintly to discern in Scripture, but that he
> always suggested those which he judged best for edifying:
> of which edification, one necessary groundwork would be,
> the securing the flock against prevailing heresies.[40]

He stressed that the importance of the Old Testament was
allegorical, and emphasised that the Old and the New were not
contradictory. Origen saw Scripture as a man, in that it is
composed of body, soul and spirit. The literal meaning of
Scripture is comprehensible to the simple; the soul, the moral
meaning, is clear to any believer when it is pointed out to him;
and the spirit is the spiritual or allegorical sense.[41] He declared,

> that the Scriptures were composed through the agency of
> God's Spirit; and they have not only the meaning which is
> clear on the surface but another meaning also which is
> hidden from most people, whereby the narrative presents
> types of certain mysteries and images of divine matters.
> Herein the whole Church is united in believing that the
> whole 'Law [i.e. the Old Testament] is spiritual' [Rom. VII,
> 14]; but this spiritual law is not perceived by all, but only
> by those on whom is bestowed the grace of the Holy Spirit
> in the word of wisdom and knowledge.[42]

So Origen was mainly concerned with the allegorical method

which enabled the inconsistencies, and, moreover, the immoralities, from a Christian point of view, of the Old Testament to be reconciled and harmonised with the Faith.

In sympathy with Origen, Keble believed that the truth about God contained in the Testaments had to be stored and reserved 'in the mystical exposition'. He called on the authority of St Chrysostom who sanctioned the Mystical Method of exposition to support his conviction. Keble thought that the initiated should, through contemplation, gradually see through the mystery of allegory and parable, and secure the reserved truth. He spoke of the importance of this method of teaching: 'I mean the way of regarding external things, either as fraught with imaginative associations, or as parabolical lessons of conduct, or as symbolical language in which God speaks to us of a world out of sight: which three might, perhaps, be not quite inaptly entitled, the Poetical, the Moral, and the Mystical phases on aspects of this visible world.' Poetry, Keble thought, was the highest form of reserve: it was the overflowing mind, relieving itself, more or less indirectly or reservedly, of thoughts and passions which most oppressed it. Each person had his own poetry; and so Christ had His poetry. Keble maintained that merely literal systems were to be suspected. He had a

... studied preference of poetical forms of thought and language, as the channel of supernatural knowledge to mankind. Poetry, traced as high as we can go, may also seem to be God's gift from the beginning, vouchsafed to us for this very purpose: at any rate the fact is unquestionable, that it was the ordained vehicle of revelation, until God Himself was made manifest in the flesh.

So, it was impossible to enjoy the full meaning of poetry without meditation. It had to be thought about carefully. Poetry made the world of sense symbolical. The symbolism had to be studied and understood. Such was symbolism in the Old Testament: its reserve had to be penetrated. And it was this meditation which Keble expected, of course, in relation to his own poetry in *The Christian Year*.

Yet more important evidence which sheds light on Keble's

religious thought is found in his preface to his edition of *The Works of Richard Hooker* (1836). The very fact that he edited Hooker's works shows that he was in some sympathy with the writer.

Hooker was a sixteenth-century Divine whose chief work was on the subject of Church government, *The Laws of Ecclesiastical Polity*. He wanted to supply the Elizabethan settlement of ecclesiastical government with a philosophical and logical basis. The Puritans made recourse only to Scripture for Christ's authority; but Hooker considered that the universe was governed by a natural law embodying God's supreme reason which was not entirely expounded in Scripture. He saw natural law as binding on men's reason, and therefore on all human institutions, both civil and ecclesiastical: 'Obedience of creatures to the law of nature is the stay of the whole world.' The Scriptures, he held, supplement natural law with a supernatural law, which furnishes man with knowledge of a future life and other mysteries of faith: 'The insufficiency of the light of nature is by the light of Scripture ... fully and perfectly supplied.'[43]

Book V of the *Laws* expounded and justified the ceremonies and ritual of the established Church. He argued that regional churches could differ in forms of government: there was nothing laid down explicitly in detail in the New Testament, and he went on to support the relationship in government between the Throne and the Church in England. This was something which Keble noted and, of course, approved: it was an essential principle of his religious thought. There was, however, no confusion between the monarch and a parliament whose elected representatives might well be agnostics or atheists at the worst.

For Keble, as well as for many others in the Church of England, Hooker displayed reverence for the deepest doctrines of the Church; he believed in the reality of sacramental grace and saw Church usages, festivals and property as all being expressions of man's sacrifice to God. Keble placed Hooker somewhere in the middle ground between Laud and Crammer, but reckoned that had he lived longer he would have got very close indeed to Laud. At any rate, Keble thought that Hooker was God's chief instrument for saving the Church from

rationalism in the sixteenth century. Similarly Keble felt that
the Church of his own time needed a defender from danger
directed from the same quarter:

> Should these volumes prove at all instrumental in
> awakening any of her children to a sense of that danger,
> and in directing their attention to the primitive Apostolical
> Church as the ark of refuge divinely appointed for the
> faithful, such an effect will amply repay the editor.[44]

Keble insisted that Hooker attributed to episcopacy a divine
origin; but perhaps Keble was reading into Hooker somewhat
more than was actually there. It is doubtful whether Hooker
meant much more than that episcopacy was a convenient,
working form of Church government which enjoyed the
sanction of history.

Nevertheless, Keble's scrupulous editorship of this major
work of a man who caught his imagination when young was a
timely and important contribution to the defence of the
principles which Keble stood for. Bowden wrote to Newman on
30 June 1836, 'Keble's Preface is most glorious.'

In 1836, as well as publishing Hooker's *Ecclesiastical Polity*,
Keble preached, in September, the Visitation Sermon in
Winchester Cathedral, which in its turn displayed much of the
content of his religious thought. He took for his subject
'Primitive Tradition recognised in Holy Scripture'. It was an
hour and a half long, and he told Newman that he had
thundered it out more emphatically than he had any sermon in
his life. He reaffirmed, in the sermon, the supremacy of the
Catholic Apostolic Church. He quoted St Paul: 'I have fought a
good fight, I have finished my course, I have kept the faith.'
The ecclesiastical writers of the age which immediately followed
the Apostles, such as Irenaeus and Tertullian, refer to the
Tradition of the whole Church, as if to something independent
of the written word, and sufficient at that time to refute heresy,
even alone. He saw, as the Fathers saw, Church tradition as
parallel to scripture. In fact, Irenaeus had written:

> By 'knowledge of truth' we mean: the teaching of the
> Apostles; the order of the Church as established from the

earliest times throughout the world: the distinctive stamp of the Body of Christ, preserved through the episcopal succession; for to the bishops the Apostles committed the care of the church which is in each place, which has come down to our own time, safeguarded without any written documents, by the most complete exposition [i.e. the Creed], which admits neither increase nor diminution [of the tradition]: the reading of the Scriptures without falsification, and consistent and careful exposition of them, avoiding temerity and blasphemy: and the special gift of love, which is more precious than knowledge, more glorious than prophecy, surpassing all other spiritual gifts.[45]

And Tertullian had explained:

[The Apostles] first bore witness to the faith in Jesus Christ throughout Judaea and founded churches there: and then went out into the world and published to the nations the same doctrine of the same faith. In the same way they established churches in every city, from which the other churches borrowed the shoot of faith and the seeds of doctrine, and are every day borrowing them so as to become churches. It is because of this that these churches are reckoned as apostolic, as being the offspring of apostolic churches. Every kind of thing must needs be classed with its origin. And so the churches, many and great as they are, are identical with that one primitive Church issuing from the Apostles, for thence they are all derived. So all are primitive, all are apostolic, while all are one. And their unity is proved by the peace they share, by the title of 'brethren', by the mutual bond of hospitality; privileges which have no other ground than the one tradition of the same revelation ... We are in communion with the apostolic churches because there is no difference of doctrine. This is our guarantee of truth. But if any of these heresies are so bold as to insert themselves into the apostolic age that they may therefore appear to have been handed down from the Apostles, because they existed under the Apostles, we can say: 'Let them display the origins of their churches; let them unroll the list of their

bishops, in unbroken succession from the beginning, so
that the first bishop of theirs shall prove to have as his
precursor and the source of his authority one of the
Apostles or one of the apostolic men, who without being an
Apostle continued with the Apostles.[46]

Keble continued in the sermon to controvert the opinion of
those who said that once the Canon of the New Testament was
complete, tradition was obsolete: the two were complementary.
He used again the well-known rule, 'Quod semper, quod ubique,
quod ab omnibus', that is, antiquity, universality and
catholicity. Tradition has helped to authorise the arrangement
of the creeds and the right interpretation of the Scriptures; and
in order to ascertain the Church's mind on discipline, and her
rites, it was necessary to consult Tradition. Implicit in the idea
of Tradition was the right to appeal to the Undivided Church,
and it was to the end a fundamental article of Keble's religious
belief. He 'thundered out' from Winchester pulpit:

Let us be only true to our sacred trust: let us put everything else by for the sake of handing down the whole
counsel of God, our good deposit, entire as we received it:
and who knows but we may by God's mercy be made
instrumental in saving the English Church from ruin.

Just as important as this sermon was for determining Keble's
religious thought, so too was the treatise he published in 1857
in defence of Archdeacon Denison who had been arraigned for
maintaining the real objective Presence in the Eucharist. This
led Keble into much the same ground as he had occupied over
the Peter Young affair. Then, Keble's campaign had been more
private and restricted than it was to be over Denison. Keble had
written to his brother on 18 July 1841, complaining of Young's
treatment. He told Thomas that Young had written to Bishop
Sumner '. . .promising to observe the Bp's directions about his
reading, and stating that his former letter was written without
communication with me and that his views were found before he
had any connection with me. And there the matter rests.'[47]
Keble went on in the same letter that Young's cause seemed to
have been prejudged and that his examination had been rigged:

It appeared like the beginning of a regular plan, for the very first paper of questions which Y. had begun with — 'State your view of the right principles to be followed in interpreting the Articles' and it was throughout on the same plan.

Later, in December 1841, Keble had reported to Thomas:

I have sent the case of Young's last rejection ... to Mr Hope in London, to know whether the Law allows of an Appeal ... I did think of solemnly protesting to the Abp. and sending a copy to each Bp. who can be at all regarded as in Communion with us: I mean protesting in the point of doctrine not at all on the point of ill-usage or oppression. I think you will see that the two grounds are quite different.[48]

And, again, on 26 January 1842, Keble showed that he had come to a decision on this principle of Church doctrine: 'I am sending the Protest today to London to Rogers to get it lithographed with all speed ... and then to send it to the Bps. as I first intended — reserving Convocation till we see whether it will be necessary.[49]

In the event, Keble had 300 copies of the Protest lithographed and he told his brother in February 1842, 'I heard today that I am blamed for continuing my Curate when the Bp. has condemned him.'

However, whereas with Peter Young's case Keble had been persuaded not to fight Sumner's decision openly and publicly, largely by the efforts of Sir John Coleridge and George Cornish, who had advised 'For Heaven's sake stand your ground in "quietness and confidence",' in the case of Denison he was prepared to prosecute his views more publicly. During Denison's hearing, both Pusey and Keble had drawn up a Protest signed by eighteen clergy which stated their belief that the doctrine of the Real Presence had been held as a point of faith from the earliest times, and that the most common view was that the wicked eat and drink unworthily of the invisible Body and Blood of Christ to their own damnation. In addition, it held that the Body and Blood of Christ, from earliest times, had been worshipped, or adored, especially at the consecration and before it had been consumed by the faithful. The Treatise was called 'On Eucharistical Adoration'. In it Keble wrote, 'It is a sad habit of thought for a theologian to train himself up in — that of instinctively adopting, out of various expositions, the most earthy and least supernatural.' He talked of the Virtual Presence, in the bread and wine, but the Real Absence of the Body and Blood of Christ. He quoted St Cyril:

> Regard not thou the Bread and Wine as merely such, for it is the Body and Blood of Christ, according to our Lord's declaration. And what if thy senses outwardly suggest the other? Yet let faith confirm thee; judge not of the matter by thy taste, but by the faith do thou assure thyself, without any manner of doubt, that He counteth thee worthy of the Body and Blood of Christ.

In support of St Cyril's view, he quoted St Ambrose and St Augustine; and went on to point out that Adoration was taken for granted by the Fathers as witnessed in Theodoret's testimony, and that of the eighth century's Church. The Liturgies have few special collects to our Lord, because the sacrifice is offered to the Father.

In Chapter IV, Keble looked to the testimony of the Reformed Church of England, where Hooker was found to uphold the Real Objective Presence in the sacrifice as well as in the sacrament. Keble explained that the reservation of the Eucharist was practised by the ancient Church, for the benefit of the sick and persecuted. Certainly, Justin Martyr wrote:

> When the president has given thanks and all the people have assented, those whom we call 'deacons' give a portion of the bread over which thanksgiving has been offered, and of the wine and water, to each of those who are present; and they carry them away to those who are absent.[50]

And both Justin Martyr and Irenaeus testified that in the second century the Eucharist used to be sent as a pledge of communion from one diocese to another. Keble maintained that the Real Objective Presence is not denied by either Articles

XXVIII or XXIX. He confirmed the XXIXth Article:

> The Wicked, and such as be void of a lively faith, although
> they do carnally and visibly press with their teeth (as
> St Augustine saith) the Sacrament of the Body and Blood
> of Christ, yet in no wise are they partakers of Christ: but
> rather to their condemnation, do eat and drink the sign of
> sacrament of so great a thing.

Finally, in support of Denison, Keble argued that it was the
duty of Churchmen, in cases such as his, to stand to their posts,
and quietly but firmly maintain their true faith. This was much
the same advice which Cornish had given eble at the time of
Young's troubles; but now there was the difference that Keble,
prepared to speak out openly, could pass on that advice to his
fellow clergymen of like principle.

Details of, and clarifications of, other important principles on
which Keble's religious thought was based may be found in his
Sermons for the Christian Year (Oxford, 1876-80). In the ones
for Lent to Passiontide, Sermon VII showed Keble's belief in
original sin: he described the little child of one day old as 'a
sinner in the sight of God': it had 'the seed and spark of original
sin'.

In Sermon IX, which was the third in a series on the subject
of confession, Keble expounded the necessity of confession and
affirmed the priest's special power to absolve. He quoted
Joshua VII, 19 and 20, and stated that sin was the mortal
disease of the soul: and he warned:

> If it be but one single Christian, committing but one
> deadly sin, in the most private and least scandalous way, it
> spreads in a mysterious way over the whole Christian
> Body: as it is written, when one member suffreth, all the
> members suffer with it, and when one member is honoured
> all the members rejoice with it.

He showed that anyone who was troubled in conscience by
some weighty matter should make special confession, as Achan
did to Joshua, and so obtain absolution from the priest, even as
Christ had promised, 'whose sins ye forgive, they are forgiven

unto them' (St John XX, 23). Likewise, Keble quoted Proverbs
XXVIII, 13: 'He that confesseth and forsaketh his sins shall
have mercy.'

Keble also recognised a very practical reason for the parish
priest why the Office of Confession should be revived. By way
of people's confession the priest could learn the true condition
of his parish. On St John's Day 1843 Keble wrote to Sir John
Coleridge:

> ... I find myself more and more oppressed with the
> consciousness of my own ignorance, and how blindly I go
> about the Parish, not knowing what men are really doing;
> and whenever I do make discoveries, they disclose a fearful
> state of things; and even when there is some seriousness,
> of respect and confidence towards the Priest as such there
> is none, or next to none. In short, our one great grievance is
> the neglect of Confession. Until we can begin to revive
> that, we shall not have the due severity in religion; and
> without a severe religion, I fear our Church will
> practically fail.[51]

Coleridge went on to record a later letter of 1844 which made
the same point: 'We go on working in the dark, and in the dark
it will be, until the rule of systematic Confession is revived in
our Church.'[52] This insistence of Keble's for the revival of
confession in the face of a very strong opposition from within
the Church of England, led Coleridge to criticise Keble.

> I own I thought Keble did unintentionally exaggerate his
> difficulties. I told him so, and that I supposed a clergyman,
> whose cure was of the manageable size of Hursley, need not
> and would not be so ignorant of the spiritual condition of
> his people, as he professed himself to be, if he brought to
> his task the requisite intelligence, industry, kindness and
> devotion; and that if he did not, it was clear he ought not
> be trusted with the delicate and difficult duty of taking
> confessions. I trusted he would gradually find the light
> dawn on him.[53]

Either Keble took the implication, or he thought that it was pointless arguing against such an attitude; undoubtedly the latter, and Coleridge was able to report that subsequently Keble seemed much happier about Hursley's parishioners. Nevertheless, as with many others of the Oxford Movement, Keble always thought of confession as an important principle of religion, all temporal, practical considerations aside.

In Sermon X, Keble recognised the frailty of human nature, but stressed God's mercy:

> ... and there are such things as secret faults, sins of infirmity, and which are not unto death: but God is just as well as merciful, and there are also open and notorious sins, grevious sins, sins mortal, and deadly sins, any of which unrepented, will be unto death.

Such then were the main principles on which Keble's religious thought rested; and to analyse them in such detail has been necessary for determining the spirit in which Keble's poetry was written. He stood in what he saw as the true tradition of the Church extending from Christ's commission to the Apostles, through the Early Fathers, through the Reformation and the Thirty Nine Articles, through Laud, through the Non-jurors, to his own days and the Oxford Movement. The Apostolic Succession, Church tradition, the authority and rule of the episcopate, were all of supreme importance to his thinking. In all of man's problems, man should make recourse to the power of God vested in the Church; and for Keble, moral considerations were always primary with him, as can be seen from his writings: indeed, the moral content, the teaching, advice and consolation, of *The Christian Year*, undoubtedly explain much of its wide appeal throughout the nineteenth century.

For Newman, perhaps, the logical conclusion of his progression from evangelicalism was to finish in the Church of Rome: not so for Keble.[54] Newman and Keble had for long been confidants and Keble had watched Newman's steps in the Rome-ward direction for many years; and he had tried to direct them elsewhere. On 30 October 1840, Keble wrote to his brother, Thomas, that he was answering an enquiry which Newman,

... has been making of me: whether he ought not to give up St Mary's. I am inclined to think on consideration, No: but I should like to know your impression, if I could, even before I write to him.

Oakley has sent word of some acquaintance of his, who having been made Romanist some 6 years ago has seen fit to return to the Church on reading Froude's Remains and some papers in B.C. [*The British Critic*] and received the Holy Communion the other day in Oakley's Chapel. I trust I am not wrong in being glad of this at a time when N. is rather getting out from an apprehension that though his arguments tell strongly against Romanism, yet the sympathies which he encourages are more strongly in favour of it.[55]

Finally the arguments, too, told strongly for Romanism so far as Newman was concerned. Keble, however, retained the firm ground of his original beliefs and consolidated the defences. True, the ground was close to Rome, but there were great obstacles between. In a letter to Newman, dated 13 May 1843, Keble wrote:

Certainly there is a great yearning ever after Rome in many parts of the Church, which seems to be accompanied with so much good that one hopes — if it be right — it will be allowed to gain strength ... I still cling to the hope you taught me to entertain, that in the present distress, where the Succession and the Creeds are, there is the Covenant, even without visible inter-Communion.[56]

Keble may have felt fellowship with the Church of Rome, but his scholarship and intellect had always convinced him of that Church's serious doctrinal errors which prevented him ever sanctioning its creed. This was reflected in all his preachings and writings, not least of all, in his poetry.

NOTES

1. Recorded by Lock, p.4.
2. Coleridge, *Memoir*, Vol. II, p.355.
3. Quoted by Stephen Neill in *Anglicanism*, London (Penguin), 1960, p.136.
4. Correspondence, C14.
5. Correspondence, C13.
6. Correspondence, C13.
7. Correspondence, C14.
8. Coleridge, *Memoir*, Vol. I, p.265.
9. G. Battiscombe, *John Keble*, London, 1963, p.190.
10. Correspondence, C15.
11. Correspondence, C15.
12. Correspondence, C15.
13. E.N.S. Thompson, *The Temple and the Christian Year*, PMLA, Vol. 54 1939, pp.1018-25.
14. Compare Newman's Tract XC. The introduction to the Tract read that it was: '... merely to show that, while our Prayer Book is acknowledged on all hands to be of Catholic origin, our Articles also, the offspring of an uncatholic age, are, through God's good providence, to say the least, not uncatholic, and may be subscribed by those who aim at being Catholic in heart and doctrine.'
15. Keble Papers, Lambeth Palace Library, Deposit 2, 34 (1824-6).
16. Keble Papers, Lambeth, Dep. 2, 36.
17. J. Keble, *Occasional Papers and Reviews*, ed. E.B. Pusey, Oxford, 1877, preface, p.ix.
18. E.L. Woodward, *The Age of Reform*, 6th ed., Oxford, 1954, p.496.
19. Thomas Hardy, *Jude the Obscure*, Papermac, 1972, pp.406-7. (First published, 1895).
20. Correspondence, C14.
21. See Appendix A.
22. J. Keble, *Sermons Occasional and Parochial*, Oxford, 1868, pp.114-15
23. Correspondence, C14.
24. Correspondence, C14.
25. Correspondence, C14.
26. Correspondence, C15.
27. Correspondence, C15.
28. *Occasional Papers and Reviews*, p.xiii.
29. Correspondence, C14.
30. Correspondence, C14.
31. Coleridge, *Memoir*, Vol. I, p.220.
32. Correspondence, C14.
33. Correspondence, C14.
34. S. Aug. *c. Faustum*, xxii. 24.
35. S. Aug: *De Libero Arbitrio*, II, 43.
36. Joseph Butler, *Analogy*, ed. W.E. Gladstone, Oxford, 1897, p.7, n.2.
37. *Occ. Papers and Reviews:* 'Warburton's Papers', p.127.
38. *Occ. Papers and Reviews:* 'Life of Sir W. Scott', p.77.
39. *Occ. Papers and Reviews*, p.77.

40. *Tracts for the Times,* 1840, 89, p.56.
41. Origen, *De Principiis,* IV, ii, 4.
42. Origen, *De Principiis,* praef. 8.
43. R. Hooker, *Laws of Ecclesiastical Polity,* Bk. II, VIII, 3.
44. R. Hooker, *The Works of,* ed. J. Keble, 2nd ed. 1841, p. cviii.
45. Irenaeus, *Adversus Haereses,* IV, XXXIII, 8.
46. Tertullian, *De Praescriptione Haereticorum,* 20, 21, 32.
47. Correspondence, C15.
48. Correspondence, C15.
49. Correspondence, C15.
50. Justin Martyr, *Apologia* I, lxv.
51. Coleridge, *Memoir,* Vol. II, pp.301-2.
52. Coleridge, Vol. II, p.302.
53. Coleridge, Vol. II, p.314.
54. See Appendix B: letter to T. Keble about Newman.
55. Correspondence, C15.
56. Quoted by Wood, p.83.

PART II

John Keble's Theory of Poetry

CHAPTER 3

Aesthetic Sense

There can be no doubt that Keble had a fine appreciation of what was beautiful, no matter whether it was displayed by the objects of Nature, or by the artefacts of man; and his sense of the beautiful necessarily governed the quality of the poetry he wrote. However he was aware of the dangers into which an overdeveloped aesthetic sense could lead people. After all, the most beautiful, and the most sublime, experience of all, was the appreciation and realisation of God: Keble had read Burke, as his *Occasional Papers and Reviews* show, and it was God who possessed a splendid yet awful terror in his omnipotence which made him the most sublime of all human conceptions.

It was this knowledge which worried Keble about the rebuilt Hursley church. Dissatisfied with the old church, and having seen the two churches at Ampfield and Otterbourne built, Keble had turned his attention to the Hursley church of which he liked only the tower. The tower remained, but the rest of the building was replaced. Keble reported to Sir John Coleridge that the days passed quickly, watching the good work in progress on the new edifice: it was a pleasure seeing the edifice grow. And in 1848, on 3 October, he commented to Thomas, his brother, as the time for the church's consecration approached:

I therefore take on myself to inform you all that our Bp. has deferred our consecration to October 24 because the Chancellor and Registrar will be engaged the week before in the Chancellor's Visitation, and of course the Church would be no Church without them. It is a nuisance, because it is bad for the people to be kept needlessly in the Barn: otherwise, I do not know that it much matters.

As for our Church, it is only too beautiful. I am sure it will and does need a strict rule to keep one from thinking to [sic] much of it in a mere aesthetic way.[1]

Beautiful, a church had to be; but not so beautiful that, in itself, it distracted attention from the worship of the awful, and most beautiful.

Even so, at the time of the consecration most of the windows were of plain glass, and it was Keble's plan to make them into a series of stained glass ones. He proposed to finance the embellishment by appealing for private gifts of windows from individuals, and by raising a fund from the many admirers of *The Christian Year.* No doubt Keble was inspired by the beautiful windows of Fairford church, and shortly the stained glass was installed, although the fund did not succeed too well and part of the expense had to be met from the profits of *The Christian Year* itself. The most famous stained-glass firm of the day made the windows from the designs of artists such as Richmond and Copley, and the whole enterprise was put under the direction of the architect Butterfield.

The result turned out to be not quite what was expected. Keble's previous anxiety was not altogether justified. One of his curates spoke of 'the sombre and devotional appearance of the whole building'. It seems that, in the end, the heavy and dark atmosphere of Victorian Gothicism was able to conquer any wayward aesthetic temptations which might have entered the congregation's hearts.

The aesthetic pleasure, however, which was to be derived from Nature was a different matter; after all, Nature was one of the ways in which God revealed himself in the world. Keble did not hesitate to pay due regard to the beauty of hills, mountains, rivers and flowers, vistas and landscapes, and it made him sad when he saw some of the effects that the industrial revolution was having on the countryside, whether it was farm machinery littering the fields, or the railway cutting across a view. In his letters to his relations and friends there are many references to what he admires in Nature, and many lyrical descriptions of journeys made which are obviously the inspiration of a poetic temperament. He wrote about the delight of gardens and flowers: he often commented to his brother on the state of his border pinks and asked after flowers he knew to be at Bisley. When he was involved in discussions about the Provostship of Oriel College in 1827, after Copleston had been translated to the Bishopric of Llandaff, it is interesting, and perhaps a little ironical, to note that one of the considerations important for Keble was that of a garden. He wrote to Thomas on 8 December 1827, from Fairford where he was curate to his father:

> You see friend Cop. is really going away from Oriel, and we are all at 6's and 7's about who is to be Dr. in his place, i.e. about 5 of the fellows have signified to me their wish that I would. 3 have said as much to Hawkins, and 5 are undeclared ... I am inclined to say upon consideration of all matters public and private, Gentlemen I thank you but Mr Hawkins had better be the man. My Father says if the majority want you take it by all means, and Elizabeth says do as you like best, it's no very great duty one way or the other — now I will tell you a thing or two which I can't so well say much of to them — if it stood in a garden I should like it much better, it would then be pleasant for them to come and visit me ... in short it is very reasonably comfortable here and I am not sure it would be comfortable there.[2]

In the event, Keble resigned the competition in favour of Hawkins for more public and important reasons other than the private consideration of a garden to the Provost's lodgings. Some of his most respected friends were against him: Newman advised his colleagues that they were electing 'not an angel but a Provost'.

The beauty of Nature gave itself to Keble's view not only in the confined space of the garden: its wider aspect was never far from Keble's mind, and from his earliest letters, as well as from his poetry, this is perfectly obvious in his vivid, lyrical and enthusiastic descriptions of his journeys or surroundings. Writing to Thomas from Fairford in 1834, he concluded a letter: 'Well here is the rain coming sweetly down and surely all the trees and flowers and grass are chirping for joy.'[3] And in 1835 he wrote from Barmouth: 'At this point we stopped, the breakers so much round as that we really felt as if we were out at sea; and the whole was more aerial or rather lunar than anything I ever saw in my born days.'[4] In 1840 Keble and his wife visited Ireland, and part of the journey, and the voyage from Holyhead to Ireland, he described to Thomas: as they approached Holyhead by road:

> The only things pretty were the grey and stained rocks
> continually peeping out, and veins of Mona marble ... We
> waited for the Mail ¼ of an hour, and when we stood off
> there was a most exquisite gleam and such a rainbow as I
> never saw before — it seemed as if the centre of it could not
> be more than 90⁰ from the sun, and besides a second
> rainbow almost as fine as the first, it appeared as if the
> first from the place where it touched the water was very
> slightly diverging into three, like two arches springing
> from the same point — the colours were repeated more or
> less distinctly three times, until the whole faded upwards
> into the misty sky: this was a promising token, and so it
> proved for though the wind got rather westerly, and a
> considerable fog arose, the rain was nothing to signify and
> the sea rolled very little. None of us was sea-sick, except
> Tom[5] a very little.

The voyage ended at Kingstown in Ireland and Keble went on:

> After we had looked at all this till 11 o'clock we got into a
> railway carriage and were whisked to Dublin in no time
> through Blackrock and what seemed to be 2 or 3 other
> bathing-places, miserably cut through by this rail-road,
> as if one should make a road 30 yds in front of the beach at
> Cowes, just where one likes poking among the rocks at low
> water.

There followed a description of the Wicklow hills, ironic because
although the railway offended Keble's aesthetic sense, it was
also able to afford him an unrivalled view of the hills.
Eventually the journey ended in Dublin which proved not quite
so attractive:

> Dublin is most of it built of brick, and is more like London
> than I expected: one of the chief differences is the cars and
> another the number of bare-footed people you see. Also
> one sees or one fancies one sees how much the are infected
> with Politics.[6]

Here Keble was getting on to common ground with Carlyle: although Carlyle dismissed Newman, Keble and Pusey as having but 'the brains of rabbits', certainly Carlyle would have agreed with Keble when he continued to upbraid the Irish as being discontented and quarrelsome, an unpleasant contrast 'with the Welch manner'.

The summer of 1842 saw Keble in the Lake District, and there he was entranced by the scenery. He described a walk to Thomas in a letter dated 10 July 1842:

> Then we crossed a coppicy ridge on the opposite slope of which we have a fair view of some of the mountains we were making for and a half amphitheatre reaching out from them: which Charlotte stopped to sketch: then we wound down to another fall [water] and a much finer one called Colwith Force ... The Langdale Pikes, the finest formed of this set of mountains, soon overhung us: we passed Blea Tarn, wch. is a place described in the Excursion and compared to an Urn: and by a long stony descent, a very wild, savage scene, into Great Langdale, which is a reach of meadows between Lingmere and the Pikes ... You go down a chasm in the side of the mountain and look up and see the water (not much of it) coming over about 50 ft. or less perpendicular: a good way above it again a block had fallen in and had been caught in the chasm so that it looks a little like a subterranean fall: this is called Dungcon Ghyll.[7]

From this sort of evidence it is clear that Keble was keenly aware of, and appreciative of, the beauties of Nature. Elsewhere, he had shown that both Nature and man could combine to reflect God and his creation's beauty: often artefacts, and especially, of course, churches, were improved by the setting of surrounding Nature. On 19 August 1840 Keble wrote to Sir John Coleridge describing the church at Llanberis: he went into details of its architecture and then made the observation, 'and all this in the midst of the most glorious sights and sounds in nature'.[8] Thus the beauty of man's handiwork could be embellished by Nature.

Similarly, Keble felt the same way about some of the old English abbeys. He wrote to Thomas on 19 July 1820:

... I wanted to see Fountains' Abbey which is within 3 miles of Ripon and I had given Davison reason not to expect me till tomorrow or next day. And right glad I am that I did so: for I am more delighted with Fountains than with any other sight to which this tour has yet introduced me: not that I like it better than Tintern: on the whole I do not think it quite so satisfactory, but it is the only thing I ever seen like it. In dimensions it is, I believe, superior, and it has its tower standing and a great part of the monastery, whereas Tintern has only the Church: the consequence that this is to a mere antiquary is far the more curious: indeed it carries you back into the domestic life of the monks most completely: but from this very circumstance you have a mixture of impressions, whereas at Tintern everything conspires to produce one single effect — add to this that the ground plan of Tintern is much more simple, tho the architecture is more modern, than that of this place: but more of it when we meet, for really and truly it is not a place to be scrawled over in a hurry.[9]

Such was the exhilaration and infatuation which Keble derived from these old abbeys. Later, he went with Hurrell Froude to Tintern and his intoxication was just as strong. Again he commented to Thomas in a letter dated 1 August 1825:

Froude and I had a very pretty tour the beginning of last week, which I suppose is the reason for my not writing to you before ... Tuesday up the river to Tintern — you must go again for the sake of boating it ... We slept at Tintern and Froude literally lost his heart to the abbey.[10]

This evidence shows the sort of man Keble was. He was no pure aesthete, and yet he recognised in hills and trees, flowers and grass, mountains and sea, the terrible beauty of God. Always the presence of God in the objects of Nature was of paramount importance. For Keble, aesthetics were allied to morals: what was beautiful was good and was of God. There was never any question of an abandonment to more sensual ecstasy in the beauty that surrounded him. He was always aware of a moral force at work, and his intellect never surrendered to the seduction of purely hedonistic appeals.

His feelings about beauty, his feelings about nature, and his feelings about God, were all embodied in his poetry, and it quickly becomes apparent that Keble's ruling idea of the close alliance between Poetry and Religion (see p.90ff) overbears all other aspects of his verse. He blended characteristics from many sources: it is easy to hear the ring of Milton, Spenser or Wordsworth in his poems: sometimes there is an imitation of Gray, sometimes a hint of the eighteenth-century gardener poets. Nevertheless, his poetry had very definite, and distinctive theories lying beneath it, which were closely associated with aesthetics and morals.

It is in Keble's Oxford University lectures which he delivered when he was Professor of Poetry between 1832 and 1841, that his poetic theories are shown most clearly. The great authors of the Classics, especially Homer and Virgil, and the Bible, particularly the Old Testament, were important serious influences on the formation of his views. As early as 1825, two years before the publication of *The Christian Year* he had published a review called 'Sacred Poetry'[11] in the *Quarterly Review* which critically assessed *The Star in the East and other Poems* by Josiah Conder, and which led Keble into a general discussion on the nature of sacred poetry; after discussing many English poets, foremost among them Milton and Spenser, Keble concluded that, 'To Spenser therefore, upon the whole, the English reader must revert, as being, pre-eminently, the sacred poet of his country': Spenser it was who fulfilled most exactly 'the general end of all his book', which was 'to fashion a gentleman, or noble person, in virtuous and gentle discipline'.

In addition to 'Sacred Poetry', Keble had published a review of Copleston's 'Praelectiones Academicae' in the *British Critic* 1814; and although Copleston was unable to complete his term as Professor of Poetry, much of what he had said appealed to Keble and gained his approval. Keble was pleased with Copleston's view on the nature of poetic criticism, that 'Her business is to enumerate rather than to demonstrate: her axioms are drawn from the feelings not the reason.' On the other hand, Keble disagreed with Copleston, in part, over poetical pleasure arising from direct description. In the review

Keble quoted some precise description from verses of Lucretius[12] in which he said '... we cannot feel any poetry'. Keble concluded: 'If this be poetry, any man may be a poet, who will take the trouble of putting a few pages of Newton's 'Opticks' into blank verse.'

Certainly there can be no doubt that Keble had thought about the nature of poetry, both in abstract terms, and in practical terms, before his lectures. Not that the lectures came easily to him: they were hard work for him, not only in the matter of content, but also in the matter of the Latin in which to compose them. Keble's letters to Thomas clearly show this (see p.77). There are continual references to the lectures throughout the term of his Professorship which show how busy he was with many other projects and duties besides. On two unspecified dates in 1834 he reported 'I have put off my Lecture till then ...' and later 'I have writ my 2 lectures and nearly writ out one of them ...' Even later in 1834, he wrote that: 'I've done my X lecture and 4/5 of the XI so I hope in a day or two to be free for Rose and Hooker and Newman — but work thickens so that one mustn't reckon on anything of the kind.'[13] On the early date in 1835, he reported to Thomas: 'The rest of the week I must stay here [Fairford] and work hard at my lecture, which I have fixed for March 3, quite forgetting that the next day is Ash Wednesday.'[14] And on 3 June 1839, he wrote: 'My lecture is all done and I am very hot on the Chrysostom which is (they say) to be out in July.'[15] Later, on 30 October 1840, he told his brother:

> I am just now getting hurried again, about sermons and lectures etc. The Poetry Lecture for the term is done; that is one good thing; but I have not yet even begun the Mysticism one, however I have set about preparing the first of that set for the Press ...[16]

From these letters, Keble's busy life becomes apparent: he mixed the duties of priest, professor and poet to a remarkable degree so that one role was never exclusive of the others. Nevertheless, the sense of urgency which can be detected in some of the letters, and the demands of a very full life, also prompted quite often a mood of relief when a task was finished.

Even though the lectures did prove hard work, much of the preparation for them had been done in Keble's previous thinking about the nature and purpose of poetry. Not only do the reviews show this, but *The Christian Year* shows that various influences had been at work on Keble's mind both in the matter of what should be the substance of poetry, and in the matter of form and diction. The influence of many English poets, the Cavalier poets, Milton, Spenser, Watts, Gray and Wordsworth among them, is obvious. The poem for the second Sunday after Easter from *The Christian Year* has the Miltonic ring about it:

> O for a sculptor's hand,
> That thou might'st take thy stand,
> Thy wild hair floating on the eastern breeze,
> Thy tranc'd yet open gaze
> Fix'd on the desert haze,
> As one who deep in heaven some airy pageant sees.

George Saintsbury wrote that the poem for the Twenty-third Sunday after Trinity is 'the only thing in the manner of Gray's Elegy that has ever come near the Elegy itself'.[17]

> Red o'er the forest peers the setting sun,
> The line of yellow light dies fast away
> That crown'd the eastern copse: and chill and dim
> Falls on the moor the brief November day.
>
> Now the tir'd hunter winds a parting note,
> And Echo bids good-night from every glade;
> Yet wait awhile, and see the calm leaves float
> Each to his rest beneath their parent shade.

And it is the Epiphany and Easter poems which are especially notable as nature poems bearing the obvious influence of Wordsworth:

> Go up and watch the new-born rill
> Just trickling from its mossy bed,
> Streaking the heath-clad hill,
> With a bright emerald thread.[18]

It is obvious from Keble's correspondence that he never liked
to publish anything that he had written without it being passed
as fit and proper by some of those who knew him well. There are
references of him sending copies of sermons to Newman or
Pusey so that they might pass judgement before they were
delivered or printed. The *Praelectiones* were sent to Christopher
Wordsworth for his comment and opinion. And, so far as
criticism of his poetry was concerned, the letters show that later
on Keble liked to know Thomas's opinion of his poetry. The
matters of rhythm and metre were important parts of poetry,
and Thomas's undated letter from Bisley makes this clear:

My Dear Charles,[19]
   If it is decided by all good judges, that 'wide waters' here
is better than 'broad waters' — then I am contented to give
up all pretensions to an *Ear for Rhythm*. To my thinking
'ask broad waters proudly spann'd' is one of the lines that
can least endure being touched — but if you think
otherwise as I said before, I allow you the casting vote.

... [To make one more remark on the ode and it shall be
positively the last.]

Everybody will begin reading (as Bessy did just now)

      'When our days are days of old'
and so tumble over, break their shins, and have to back
and begin again.

So, Tom Keble's criticism on the 'Ode for the Encaenia at
Oxford, on the Installation of the Duke of Wellington, 1834',
was sought but not heeded. The published version retains,
despite Bessy and Thomas, 'When ours are days of old', and
'wide waters'.
   Even this poem, largely reminiscent of noble and martial
exploits, has its Wordsworthian touches';

    Where hoary cliffs of Lusitane
    Like aged men, stand waiting on the shore,
    And watch the setting sun, and hear th'Atlantic roar

and the mountain gale that:

> O'er many a deep monastic vale,
> O'er many a golden river loves to fling,
> His gatherings from the thymy lap of spring.

Of all the poets in the history of English literature, Wordsworth exerted the most serious influence on Keble. Keble regarded Wordsworth, laureate from 1843 to 1850, as the best poet of the age and one of the important voices among the English bards. In turn, too, it is certain that Keble's Christian poetry had considerable effect on Wordsworth's later work. The relationship is a crucial one in studying both Keble's poetic theories and his poetry.

NOTES

1. Correspondence, C15.
2. Correspondence, C13.
3. Correspondence, C14.
4. Correspondence, C14.
5. No doubt Keble's nephew, son of Thomas, who must have accompanied the Kebles to Ireland.
6. Correspondence, C15.
7. Correspondence, C15. Georgina Battiscombe, in *John Keble*, London, 1963, p.230 wrongly transcribes much of this letter: for instance, she reads 'stretch' for 'reach', and 'Lingmell' for 'Lingmere'. Also, there are omissions which she does not signify, such as 'and compared to an Urn' after 'The Excursion'.
8. Coleridge, *Memoir*, Vol. II, p.363.
9. Correspondence, C13.
10. Correspondence, C13.
11. Printed in *Occasional Papers and Reviews*.
12. *Occasional Papers and Reviews*, p.157.
13. Correspondence, C14.
14. Correspondence, C14.
15. Correspondence, C14.
16. Correspondence, C15.
17. *Cambridge History of English Literature*, Cambridge, 1953. Vol. XIII, p.170.
18. 'Monday in Easter Week', *The Christian Year*, Oxford, 1827.
19. Correspondence of Thomas Keble, Keble College Library, C19. Thomas often addressed John as Charles in his letters: perhaps a light-hearted allusion to John's respect for Charles, King and Martyr.

CHAPTER 4

Keble and Wordsworth

Keble had been introduced to Wordsworth's poetry, when he was a young undergraduate at Corpus Cristi College, Oxford. Keble was there in 1806; and in 1809, John Taylor Coleridge, later a prominent High Court judge arrived there. He was the son of Samuel Taylor Coleridge's brother James, and he took to Corpus with him copies of *The Lyrical Ballads* and Wordsworth's *Poems in Two Volumes.* Apart from John Coleridge, it does not seem probable that any of the Corpus undergraduates had known Wordsworth's poetry before going up to the University. Later, John Coleridge, who was to become the first biographer of John Keble, wrote that the influence of Wordsworth's poetry undoubtedly played upon Arnold, one of the Corpus group, bringing out in him his great, lofty and imaginative ideas. No doubt it was Wordsworth's inspiration that drove him, when the headmaster of Rugby School, to take reading parties of senior boys to the Lake District, in order to seek spiritual refreshment away from the industrial towns during the vacations.

Keble became a great admirer of Wordsworth as his poetry clearly shows. It is interesting that Wordsworth's *Ecclesiastical Sketches* were published in 1822. He was not concerned with writing about the doctrines of the Christian faith. As Wordsworth wrote to Henry Alford on 21 February 1840, talking about the discussion of religious doctrine in poetry as a whole, he felt 'far too deeply to venture on handling the subject as familiarly as many scruple not to do'.[1]

It is impossible to believe that Wordsworth was in any way adversely criticising Keble for the publication of *The Christian Year.* It is more likely that Wordsworth was aware that Keble was competent in dealing with doctrine and liturgy in poems while others were not. It was always the rhythm, metre and language that Wordsworth condemned: never the content. Indeed Wordsworth admired *The Christian Year* so much that he declared, 'It is very good; so good, that if it were mine, I would write it all over again'; and it was Pusey's opinion that Wordsworth and Keble should jointly recast the poetry.

Two other sources support the view that Wordsworth admired the content of Keble's poetry. Henry Crabb Robinson wrote that Sara Coleridge had noted in her copy of the *Memoir* of Wordsworth that she herself 'heard Wordsworth declare that there is better poetry in Watts than in Keble'. Crabb Robinson also stated that he had heard Wordsworth 'speak slightingly of the mechanical talents of Keble, but he esteemed the tendency of his poems'. And Wordsworth himself wrote to his nephew Christopher in 1836 saying that he had analysed Keble's 'verses on baptism' and had proved the style: '... how vicious it was in diction, though the thoughts and feelings were quite suitable for the occasion. Keble has been seduced into many faults by his immoderate admiration of the ancient classics.'[2]

As it happens, although Keble owed much to Wordsworth in the composition of *The Christian Year,* it is undoubtedly true that Wordsworth himself owed something to Keble in his later work concerned with devotional and religious themes.

At no time was the relationship between Keble and Wordsworth close or intimate. There are references to Wordsworth in Keble's letters to Thomas, but they are mostly passing ones, or trivial. On 3 June 1815, he mentioned to Thomas, in a letter mainly concerned with telling about the manufacture of a wooden leg for their sister Elizabeth: 'Wordsworth is here [Oxford] and I am to go with Coleridge some day to see him. My review I see is out, and Coleridge has told him of it: which I had rather he had not, being as how I talk about his being childish etc.'[3] In 1825 Keble wrote to Thomas about a friend of theirs called Jack Menzies who had just sent a letter to John. Menzies was 'in as much of a passion as ever I knew him cause why he has not been writ to so long'. Keble reported that Menzies '... has been touring in the Lakes, and saw Wordsworth in a plaid jacket which was very surprising'.[4] Much later, in 1842, Keble wrote to Thomas from Low Wood, near Ambleside, on 25 July: 'I suppose I shall call on Wordsworth tomorrow: we are not 3 miles from him I believe.'[5]

However, while the relationship was not intimate, Keble's great respect for Wordsworth's poetry is evident throughout his work, and throughout his life. There was one period of brief correspondence between the two at the time when Keble was a tutor of Oriel College and Wordsworth was seeking admission for his son John at Oxford. Wordsworth's letters to Keble are in Keble College Library; and Keble's are in the collection of Dove Cottage Papers. It may be true, however, that one reason for Keble's reluctance to publish *The Christian Year* in 1827 was partly due to Wordsworth's indirect influence. In Wordsworth's poem 'The Liturgy' he denied having the power or the possibility of writing on the basic precepts of the Christian faith. The 'stupendous mysteries' were not within the bounds of his poetic gifts:

> Upon that circle traced from sacred story
> We only dare to cast a transient glance,
> Trusting in hope that Others may advance
> With mind intent upon the King of Glory,
> From his mild advent till his countenance
> Shall dissipate the seas and mountains hoary.

Mary Moorman, Wordsworth's biographer, writes that: '... the answer to this challenge came in 1827, in the publication of Keble's *Christian Year* — which for the next half-century was unrivalled as a book of devotion in Anglican households'. It is more likely though that Keble was put off publishing his poems by what Wordsworth had written; by all accounts he was a modest, and retiring man, and he took much persuading by his friends, especially Davison, and by his father, before he would publish — and even then he did so anonymously. The book was not only popular in Anglican households, but elsewhere as well: Newman's 'fons et origo mali' had a universal appeal, for dissenters as well as High Churchmen.

While the cause for Wordsworth's complaints against Keble's poetry can easily be recognised in Keble's archaic diction and often tortured syntax, it can also be appreciated both from Keble's poetry and his lectures that Keble thought much the same as Wordsworth over poetic inspiration. Indeed, much of what Keble wrote is a restatement of Wordsworth's Preface to the second edition of *The Lyrical Ballads,* published in 1800.[6]

Wordsworth's famous passage

> I have said that poetry is the spontaneous overflow of
> powerful feelings: it takes its origin from emotion
> recollected in tranquillity: the emotion is contemplated till,
> by a species of reaction, the tranquillity gradually
> disappears, and an emotion, kindred to that which was
> before the subject of contemplation, is gradually produced,
> and does itself actually exist in the mind.

accords with Keble's stipulation in Lecture XXII that poetry
must be the 'spontaneous outburst of the poet's inmost feeling',
though tempered by a due reserve and recourse to rhyme and
metre; and in Lecture IV Keble had already made his
distinction between poets of primary rank, and poets of
secondary rank, in which primary poets are 'spontaneously
moved by impulse' and 'resort to composition for relief and
solace of a burdened or overwrought mind'.[7]

It is clear enough, however, that Wordsworth's influence
must have been strong on Keble in the years before 1832 when
he was elected to the Chair of Poetry. Then, despite his views on
poetry obvious from his occasional reviews, and what was
apparent from his own poetry, Keble found it necessary to think
deeply about the nature of poetry and to write down his
opinions in lecture form. As previously mentioned he did not
find it a particularly easy task.

Sir John Coleridge records how Keble saw his way with
difficulty into the term of office.[8] He quoted from a letter sent
to him by Keble:

> I am not particularly sanguine about this Professorship, to
> which my friends have been so kind as to nominate me;
> I feel as if the Latin wouldn't come; and what is worse, I
> have not come to any resolution on the subject to lecture
> on; if anything occurs to you, the smallest donation will be
> thankfully received.

It was not long before he had decided on his theme for the
lectures, and, as John Coleridge pointed out, he had touched on
it in a letter to Froude as early as September, 1825, when
writing of *The Christian Year*. Keble wrote with his usual

modesty:[9]

> It would be a great delight to do something, which might
> be of use to the sort of persons you mention: but that must
> be left for someone who *can* do it — and probably whenever
> it is done, it will be done, it will be done by somebody who
> never thought of it himself, but merely wrote to relieve his
> own mind. Indeed, that was the original purpose of what
> you have seen, and so far it has proved very useful; but
> there is no making a silk purse out of a sow's ear — a
> foolish figure, but farewell that.[10]

So he showed that the poet wrote from a full heart which
overflowed in order to relieve itself, much in accord with
Wordsworth's ideas about the origin of poetry.

Even so, when it came to rationalising what he thought about
poetry the task looked formidable, and the preparation was
hard work. Keble wrote to Sir John Coleridge on 13 February
1832: 'I was at Oxford the beginning of this week "reading in",
— it is uphill work to me, and you never said a much truer thing
than when you told Tom I was ten years too old for the task.' In
a similar vein, Keble wrote to his brother Tom in what must
have been early 1832. The letter is undated:

> I have writ 1/3 or more of the first lecture, but can hardly
> tell how it may do. I mean to consider Ποιητική [11]
> as affording relief to a full mind, in which single point of
> view I apprehend there is enough *sayable* on it to fill
> 20 lectures easily if one had the sense to find it out,
> and also the Latin to say it in.

And again to Tom, he remarked: 'N.B. The smallest donations
either of sense or Latin will be thankfully received.'[12]

The business of composing and delivering the lectures in
Latin was not a prospect which Keble relished: this is clear
from his letters, too.

To Sir John Coleridge he wrote (in a letter already quoted):

> ... and as to the Latin it will be, it will be ἀγαπητόν,[13]
> if I do not disgrace myself. However, I do not like the

notion of making it English, even if the Doctors would allow it; because of the moral certainty of a large importation of trash, which ought not to be on the University account; and also because I think Latin would suffer more than Poetry would gain.

No doubt, too, the idea of keeping the lectures in Latin had much to do with the doctrine of Reserve which was very important in Keble's theory of poetry. The use of Latin meant that the ideas he was putting forward were not available to the vulgar and the uninitiated: there was no reason for the lectures to be popular: after all, they were about poetry, closely allied to religion, and therefore demanded reverence and a due amount of reserve. When occasion demanded, Keble was well aware of the disadvantage of using Latin as a means of communication. When he had composed the Protest over Peter Young's rejection, he sent a copy to Thomas, and wrote on 23 December 1841: 'I am afraid Charlotte's notion about doing it in Latin, though very nice in many respects, would have the effect of putting the thing on the shelf.'[14] With the lectures, it was not a case of putting them 'on the shelf', but of reserving what was said for those who were able to appreciate it, and for the *cognoscenti*. It was left to Matthew Arnold, when he filled the Chair later, to throw over the Latin traces and deliver his famous lectures, for the first time, in English. And so, bound up with Keble's commitment to lecturing in Latin was his recognition and acceptance of the doctrine of Reserve, not only in its relation to religion but also in relation to poetry, which, in any case, he regarded as allied to religion, if not indeed an integral part of it. In Lecture XL, Keble wrote '... real Religion is in striking accord with true poetry', and later, in the same lecture, he saw it as 'a high-born handmaid' that 'may wait upon and minister to true Religion'.[15] He thought that if the lectures were given in English, the sacred subject of poetry might have been infected by a popular and vulgar interest. To maintain Latin was to keep the subject properly esoteric: subsequently it might be judged what should be communicated to the people in general. Keble saw in Latin the means of curbing popular extravagance. He considered that there were many men in the field of literary criticism who were pretentious, and that many of them were responsible for troublesomely insistent publications: some of these publications were even weekly. He regarded Latin as being the medium of good taste, which provided a kind of veil against the intrusions of pernicious opinion.

Nevertheless, the composition of Latin made his task difficult, and as is seen from his letters, he valued any help which might have been offered from his friends. The result was successful and his forebodings short-lived. Newman praised the Lectures: 'As coming from a person of high reputation[16] for Latinity they were displays of art.'[17] and: 'His greatest literary work, his Lectures on Poetry so full of acute remark and so beautiful in language, is in Latin.'[18]

However, having resigned himself to Latin, and briefly outlined the theme of his lectures to Thomas Keble in early 1832, he was much fuller in explanation when he wrote to Sir John Coleridge in February 1832. Keble gave his inaugural lecture towards the end of that month, but even so his ideas and theme expanded as time went on, as the lectures show, and led Keble into a second term of the Professorship. To Coleridge, on 13 February Keble wrote:

My notion is, to consider Poetry as a vent for overcharged feelings, or a full imagination, and so account for the various classes into which poets naturally fall, by reference to the various objects which are apt to fill and overpower the mind, so as to require a sort of relief. Then there will come in a grand distinction between what I call Primary and Secondary Poets; the first poetising for their own relief, the second for any other reason. Then I should βασανιζειν [19] one after another each of the great Ancients, whom in my Royal Authority I think worthy of the name of a Primary Poet, and show what class he belongs to, and what sort of person I take him to have been. From which will arise certain conclusions as to the degree in which the interest of poetry depends on the character of the writer, as shewn in his works; and again, as to the relation between this art, and practical goodness, moral and religious.[20]

The similarity between the views on poetry of Wordsworth and Keble has already been stated, but here again the idea of poetry being the means of relief for overcharged feelings is consistent with Wordsworth's theories. Keble's reverence towards Wordsworth, though rarely expressed as such, is perfectly obvious. The Lectures on Poetry were dedicated to him:

> To William Wordsworth, true philosopher and inspired poet who by the special gift and calling of Almighty God whether he sang of man or of Nature failed not to lift up men's hearts to holy things nor ever ceased to champion the cause of the poor and simple and so in perilous times was raised up to be a chief minister not only of sweetest poetry but also of high and sacred truth. This tribute slight though it be, is offered by one of the multitude who feel ever indebted for the immortal treasure of his splendid poems in testimony of respect, affection, and gratitude.

After such a dedication, it is not surprising that Keble's lectures bear the mark of Wordsworth's poetic theories.

Later in 1839, when Wordsworth was received by the University in Oxford, Keble as Professor of Poetry was called on to give the Creweian Oration. When Wordsworth arrived for the conferment of his honorary degree, he listened to Keble's praises:

> But I judged, Gentlemen of the University, that I should satisfy, and more than satisfy, what this topic demands if only I should recall to your recollection him (specially now as in this honourable circle which surrounds me he is himself present,) who of all poets, and above all has exhibited the manners, the pursuits, and the feelings, religious and traditional, of the poor, — I will not say in a favourable light merely, but in a light which glows with the rays of heaven. To his poetry, therefore, they should, I think, be now referred, who sincerely desire to understand and feel that secret and harmonious intimacy which exists between honourable Poverty, and the severer Muses, sublime Philosophy, yea, even, our most holy Religion.[21]

Though Wordsworth was gratified by this tribute at the end of Keble's oration, it seems curious that Keble should identify Wordsworth particularly as the poet of the poor. It is true that he had been a radical, which led to some second thoughts on the Kebles' part when the Lectures were about to be published. Keble wrote to his brother on 23 January 1844:

> You see the Praelectiones are now all in print and they are waiting only for the Index, Title and Preface. Now I have always intended to write a few lines of dedication to old Mr. Wordsworth: but Mrs. J.K. has started a doubt on account of his having begun life as a Radical. You must give me your unbiased opinion soon, for I want with all speed to write it and send it to C. Wordsworth to be criticized, unless someone dissuades me.[22]

So far as Wordsworth's youthful poverty was concerned, it might have been honourable, but it was not the sort of poverty which afflicted and oppressed Goody Blake. In the sense that Wordsworth was the poet of such characters as Goody Blake, and the Female Vagrant, Keble's statement was true; but perhaps the oration was one occasion when Keble was being over sententious and moralistic. Yet it still showed his great respect for Wordsworth.

Still more important in showing the consistent influence which Wordsworth's thoughts and poems had on Keble, is the motto chosen for *Lyra Innocentium* published in 1846, and subtitled *Thoughts in verse on Christian Children; their ways and their privileges.* The motto was the last stanza of Wordsworth's 'Anecdote for Fathers':

> O dearest, dearest boy! my heart
> For better lore would seldom yearn,
> Could I but teach the hundredth part
> Of what from thee I learn.

This poem, of course, is very appropriate and important in understanding Keble's theory of poetry; and it agrees very much with what Keble wrote elsewhere. In Wordsworth's poem, the adult tries to force the boy to rationalise his preference for Kilve rather than Liswyn Farm. The boy is unable, or unwilling, to do this, and finally, in order to satisfy the adult, casts around for some explanation that will stand as a reason for the insistent adult. He sees the weather-vane on Liswyn Farm and gives it as a negative reason for preferring Kilve by the seashore. The point, however, that Wordsworth was making, was that the boy's feelings for a place should have been sufficient for the adult: there was no need for reasons. What the poem states takes us back to Keble's review of Copleston's *Praelectiones,* already quoted, in which he stated that poetic criticism's 'axioms are drawn from the feelings, not the reason'.

In a number of other places, too, Keble referred directly to poems of Wordsworth. In his review of Lockhart's *Life of Sir Walter Scott,*[23] which is particularly interesting for showing more of what Keble thought about other contemporary poets, Keble reinforced his theory that ordinary and uneducated people were capable of poetical experience. He wrote:

The quiet and domestic character will be recognized as poetical, when, being cast upon the turmoil of busy life, it betrays itself to be forever contriving imaginary escapes and little images of the repose for which it longs: the animated and soaring temper in like manner, when untoward circumstances keep it still in the shade and it manages to relieve itself by the same sort of indirect exercise.

Keble then went on to quote from 'The Reverie of Poor Susan', Wordsworth's poem about a girl from the country disorientated from her proper surroundings, isolated and alienated in London:

The former will sympathise with those who in a great city cherish in secret the remembrance of their native mountains: —

Bright volumes of vapour through Lothbury glide,
And a river flows on down the vale of Cheapside.

Keble concluded that it was the difficulty, and the way, of overcoming the person's desperate longing for the old, habitual scenes, which marked such a character as Susan as poetical. It will be seen later, in Part III, that similar sentiments are echoed in Keble's own poetry, for example in the Morning Hymn, and the poem for St Matthew.

Later, in the same review Keble wrote of Scott's childhood, and showed how Lockhart described Scott's boyhood and youth having a great influence on his writings. Keble noted: 'Nowhere, probably, in biography can be found a completer illustration of Wordsworth's sentiment, 'The child is father of the man'. Wordsworth wrote about the sentiment in the lines beginning 'My heart leaps up when I behold ...', but the last three lines of that poem were used as a sort of introduction to his great Immortality Ode. This ode Keble indirectly referred to in Lecture XXXIX when he was discussing the ancient, Pythagorean theory of souls coming from an unknown region before birth and the Platonic theory of recollection. Without naming Wordsworth or the ode, Keble wrote:

> The finest poem of the greatest poet within our times is mainly based on this belief: namely, that our recollections of childhood are touched with their peculiarly exquisite and far-reaching charm, simply because of its dim feeling of a former existence and of a life closer to divine influence.

There could hardly have been better praise for a poem, or a poet: not even Walter Scott, before he gave up poetry because of Byron's competition,[24] earned that admiration.

Keble himself took childhood as a theme for *Lyra Innocentium: Thoughts in verse on Christian children, their ways and their privileges* (1846), in which a poem such as 'Children like Parents' reflects a combined Wordsworthian and analogical view of babies:

> And even as loving nurses here
>   Joy in the babe to find
> The likeness true of kinsmen dear
>   Or brother good or kind,

> So in each budding inward grace
> The Seraphs' searching ken
> The memory haply may retrace
> Of ancient, holy men.

And the theme occurs often in *The Christian Year*, for example, in the poem for the Sixth Sunday after Epiphany, and 'Holy Baptism'.

Wordsworth was looked to in 'Sacred Poetry', when Keble wanted to substantiate his claim that sacred poetry must reflect a poet's sustained general tone of thought. It was part of what Keble held to be the quality of a primary poet: the primary poet had to be consistent and sustained. If a poet in his own life was fickle and his temperament continually changing, if he had flashes of brilliance only on occasions, and if his thoughts constantly fluctuated, then he did not belong to the first order. Even such a poet as Dryden was denied the first rank (see p. 92). Keble quoted 'Wordsworth's beautiful description of the Stock-dove':

> He should sing 'of love with silence blending,
> Slow to begin, yet never ending
> Of serious faith and inward glee'.[25]

Certainly, it seems, Wordsworth as poet was always in Keble's mind. In Lecture XVI Keble remarked that as fire is kindled by fire 'so a poet's mind is kindled by contact with a brother poet'; and this must have been the case for Keble, judging by the pervasive, obvious influence of Wordsworth in his poetry and his writings about poetry. As remarked before, the Lectures echo the sounds of Wordsworth's poetic philosophy: in Lecture XXII Keble stated that poetry must be 'the spontaneous outburst of the poet's inmost feelings',[26] and in XXIV Keble added that, 'The essential requirement is that everything should flow from a full heart'.[27] In Lecture XXX Keble referred to 'The Excursion', book IV, lines 717-44, and 851-87, where Wordsworth talked of the Greeks, and said that in Greece:

> ... emanations were perceived; and acts
> Of immortality, in Nature's course,
> Exemplified by mysteries ...

Yet this was one of the areas where Keble and Wordsworth began to differ. In view of Wordsworth's declared opinion that Keble had been seduced by the classics, it is difficult to see the brother poets observing the ancient authors in the same light. Keble's emphasis lay very much on the Classics as the lectures on poetry show: he saw in the work of the great classical poets the promise of what was to come in English poetry, at the same time as interpreting them, together with the Hebrew authors, in the role of primitive priests of true religion which was later to be revealed to men by the coming of Christ. As a classical scholar, therefore, it was only natural that Keble should concentrate on the poets of Greece and Rome.

The other area where there was serious disagreement between the 'brother poets' was over the matter of diction. Wordsworth's opinion of *The Christian Year* has already been noted: he felt there was much room for improvement in the modes of Keble's expression. Certainly Keble was not bothered to use 'a selection of language really used by men'.[28] Keble's language rather belonged to the stock of poetic words whose repository lay in the eighteenth century; and, beyond that, much of Keble's diction was similar to that of Milton's minor poems. It was not so grand as that of 'Paradise Lost', but it bore remarkable resemblance to that of the shorter poems. To quote Wordsworth, in another context, he no doubt thought that Keble was one of those who 'From generation to generation ... are the dupes of words';[29] but Keble would have seen in his recourse to an esoteric form of vocabulary yet another way of giving his poetry a due reserve and modesty which he believed was proper.

Where the poets did agree was in the field of rhythm and metre. In his review of Lockhart's *Life of Sir Walter Scott* Keble wrote that rhyme and metre in poetry are the necessary controls on the violent passion for expression.[30] Yet, as usual with Keble, there was another purpose, that of investing the feelings seeking expression with a due sense of reserve:

... the conventional rules of metre and rhythm may evidently have the effect of determining in some one direction, the overflow of sentiment and expression, where with the mind might otherwise be fairly oppressed. On the other hand, the like rules may be no less useful, in throwing a kind of veil over those strong or deep emotions, which need relief, but cannot endure publicity.

It is interesting that a little before in this review Keble stated that: 'Poetry is the indirect expression in words, most appropriately in metrical words, of some overpowering emotion, or ruling taste, or feeling, the direct indulgence whereof is somehow repressed.'[31]

This sentiment, so much in accord with what Wordsworth thought about poetry, was followed by the assertion 'that mountainous districts are more favourable to the poetical temper than unvaried plains, the habits of the country than those of the town, of an agricultural than of a commercial population'.[32] It is possible to see in this part of the review a direct reference to Wordsworth, and a plain statement about the sort of poetry Keble composed.

Elsewhere Keble wrote about the discipline of poetic form. In Lecture I, he defined poetry as being associated with measure and a definite rhythm of sound, at the same time as declaring that it was the means of relief for sufferers with oppressed hearts: poetry's chief aim was to recall or renew, and 'bring vividly before us pictures of absent objects'.[33] And in Lecture XXVIII Keble made sure that his listeners did not take his stress on poetic form with the wrong emphasis. Metre and rhythm were secondary: true feelings were most important. Keble made it clear that poetry:

> ... uses both words and metres as mere instruments, just like a queen employing her messengers: they are not dominant, not of first importance ... Hence it follows, with regard to any poet who by general consent is mainly praised for the richness and beauty of his diction, that we may fairly question if he has anything in common with those who are made poets by Nature and true feeling before they occupy themselves with literary style and metrical form.[34]

The difference between Keble and Wordsworth on this ground was that Wordsworth made a distinction between prose, metrical composition, and poetry, and it was unnecessary for poetry to have the bounds of metre, whereas Keble regarded metre as an integral part of poetry. Wordsworth's views were expressed in the Preface to the Second Edition of *Lyrical Ballads* 1800, where he analysed Gray's sonnet 'In vain to me the smiling mornings shine'. Exactingly, and, perhaps, somewhat pedantically, Wordsworth noted: '... it is equally obvious, that, except for rhyme, and in the use of the single word "fruitless" for fruitlessly, which is so far a defect, the language of these lines does in no respect differ from that of prose'.

However, for his own part, Wordsworth went on to state that he thought metre and rhyme were an admirable means of restraining excitement and over balanced pleasure in poetry:

If the words, however, by which this excitement is produced, be in themselves powerful, or the images and feelings have an undue proportion of pain connected with them, there is some danger that the excitement may be carried beyond its proper bounds. How the co-presence of something regular, something to which the mind has been accustomed in various moods and in a less exciting state, cannot but have great efficacy in tempering and restraining the passion by an inter-texture of ordinary feeling, and of feeling not strictly and necessarily connected with the passion.

It cannot be denied that there were differences between Wordsworth's and Keble's theories of poetry; but the main difference for Keble was implicit in a dilemma he found himself in which concerned privacy and publicity. For Keble poetry was a private affair, a form of catharsis if you wrote it, a source of possible catharsis in a vicarious way if you read it and a source of meditation and reflection. This view of poetry was too narrow for Wordsworth: poetry for him had a public duty and was not only concerned with the private, contemplative moods of Religion. A sense of social responsibility, and of man's place philosophically in his public world, occupied Wordsworth's mind more than Keble's. Both Wordsworth's poems and his various prefaces show this well enough. Keble's poetry was essentially private, narrower in theme than Wordsworth's; and, what is more important, Keble's theory of poetry was more extreme.

NOTES

1. Quoted by Mary Moorman in *William Wordsworth: A Biography*, Oxford, 1965, Vol. II, p.394.
2. Moorman, Vol. II, p.480.
3. Correspondence, C13.
4. Correspondence, C13.
5. Correspondence, C15.
6. It does not seem that Keble paid much regard to Wordsworth's ideas on poetic diction, laid out in the appendix to the Preface in the third edition, 1802.
7. John Keble's lectures on poetry — *Praelectiones Academicae* — were in Latin. E.K. Francis translated them into English and the lectures were published in that form in 1912. Quotations from the lectures will be from his translation: John Keble, *Lectures on Poetry*, tr. E.K. Francis, Oxford, 1912.
8. Coleridge, *Memoir*, Vol. I, p.207.
9. See Appendix B.
10. Coleridge, Vol. I, p.121.
11. 'poetics'.
12. Correspondence, C14.
13. 'satisfactory'.
14. Correspondence, C15.
15. J. Keble, *Lectures on Poetry*, tr. E.K. Francis, Oxford, 1912, Vol. II, p.484.
16. Keble was the second person at Oxford to take a double first, that is a first class degree in both Mathematics and Classics. The first had been Robert Peel: Keble was thought to have out-Peeled Peel.
17. J.H. Newman, *Idea of a University:* Elementary Studies, Sect. 3(2).
18. J.H. Newman in John Keble, *Occ. Papers and Reviews*, Oxford, 1877, preface, p.xii.
19. 'put to the test'.
20. Coleridge, *Memoir*, Vol. I, p.208.
21. Coleridge, *Memoir*, Vol. I, p.260. Coleridge apologises for his translation of the original Latin.
22. Correspondence, C15.
23. *Occ. Papers and Reviews*, p.10. Originally published in 'British Critic', 1838.
24. Review of *Life of Sir W. Scott*, *Occ. Papers and Reviews*, Oxford, 1877. p.73. Keble wrote that Scott left off writing in poetry because he thought Byron was better.
25. *Occ. Papers and Reviews*, 'Sacred Poetry', p.90.
26. *Lectures*, Vol. II, p.37.
27. *Lectures*, Vol. II, p.96.
28. W. Wordsworth, Preface to 2nd Edition of *Lyrical Ballads*, 1800.

29. W. Wordsworth in his *Postscript* to the poems of 1835: he was discussing Poor Law amendment, and, later, Church reform.
30. *Occ. Papers and Reviews*, p.17.
31. *Occ. Papers and Reviews*, p.6.
32. *Occ. Papers and Reviews*, p.7.
33. *Lectures*, Vol. I, p.21.
34. *Lectures*, Vol. II, p.218.

CHAPTER 5

The Nature of Poetry, and Views on Other Poets

The divine nature of poetry was the basis for all Keble's discussion about poetry; he stressed its affinity with religion and its role as interpreter of the Word of God. His own poetry was a practical attempt to show this. In the 'Preface to the Second Edition of *Lyrical Ballads* 1800', Wordsworth declared that Poetry '... can boast of no celestial ichor that distinguishes her vital juices from those of prose'. But for Keble this sort of statement was near to profanity: for Keble poetry was much more refined than Wordsworth's view of it, and it was closely identified with religion. In the review 'Sacred Poetry',[1] Keble wrote ᾿Ένθεον ἡ ποίησις ,[2] and in the Lectures Keble continually stressed the close relationship of poetry and religion. In his last Lecture, XL, he emphasised the inseparability of the two, which he had sought to show earlier. He saw poetry as the precursor of true Religion and he continually talked of Nature, and Religion, always having close at hand their handmaid, Poetry. Lecture XXX describes how the Hebrew sacred writers were the first to address themselves to poetry and song, reflecting thereby their appreciation of the charm and beauty of the world, all part of the visible glory of God: the Hebrew poets realised the Divine presence in the world around them, and saw rural charms as the evidence and image of Heavenly beauty. In Lecture XL Keble thought that no poet '... will ever be great who does not constantly spend time and toil in studying the beauty of earth and sky'.[3] Earlier, in the same lecture, he had written:

> What more conceivable than that all poetry may have been providentially bestowed on man as the first elements, the prelude, so to speak, of genuine piety? since for one thing, ancient records as a rule bear out the conclusion that there has seldom been a revival of religion unless a high and

noble order of poets has first led the way: and for
another, both in effect and in character, real Religion is
in striking accord with true poetry.[4]

Keble went on to declare that poetry prepared the way for
Theology, and pointed out that any period of great poetic
activity heralded a time of better religious spirit to come. So he
saw in the Elizabethan poets and their poetry a temper which
was exactly in accord with the 'healthier religious spirit' which
was to prevail in the reign of Charles: the Elizabethan poets, of
course, were unaware of this phenomenon. He used as a
particular example, Shakespeare:

> ... the greatest of them all, the delight of all the world,
> especially of young England, did he effect nothing, who
> sometimes by jest, sometimes by bitter satire, lashed
> chiefly those very mischiefs which, in the age immediately
> following, were to work such fatal harm in our state?[5]

Here, it is interesting to note that Keble, in Lecture V, managed
conveniently to excuse Shakespeare for his 'looser and broader
scenes'[6] because of the taste of the time: they were not to
Shakespeare's own inclination, and they were sometimes
presented by way of warning 'as drunken helots were shown to
the youth of Sparta'. With a sort of chop-logic, Shakespeare,
whom Keble classified as a primary poet, was described as
having one of the essential qualities of such a poet —
consistency; but, Keble said, it was a 'consistent in-
consistency'.[7]

Religion, then, to pursue Keble's line of thought, freely
availed itself 'of every comfort Poetry can give it'. The two were
bound inexorably together by 'a tone of modest and religious
reserve'. As in religion, the doctrines of reserve held sway in
poetry: as laid down in Holy Scripture 'things of highest worth
should for the most part not be offered to listless and
unprepared minds'.[8]

It was those writers of a devout and religious sense who were
most likely to turn out to be poets. In Lecture XXVIII, Keble
wrote that 'true Poetry' was 'most likely to be found in men
whose minds are thoroughly imbued with sacred prophecy and

history';[9] and he always talked of poetry as being a divine gift, or divinely inspired. In Lecture I, he considered 'the glorious art of Poetry a kind of medicine divinely bestowed upon man'.[10] and in Lecture XXII he referred to the 'divine name of poet'[11] In Lecture XXXV, he repeated one of his favourite themes that poetry had been a divine substitute, or preparation, in the early history of man: it had existed, and, indeed, still exists, as a solace for unhappy and sorrowing mortals: it represented that spiritual anodyne 'till such time as true Religion should be revealed'.[12]

So far as Keble was concerned, there was no doubting that divine ichor was instilled into poetry. Nevertheless, all poets were not to be thought of as of the same quality. He made an important, fundamental and essential distinction between poets of Primary rank, and poets of Secondary rank; and what marks the Primary poet is the expression of his feelings, not the command of his reason. Poets, Keble reckoned, are born not made. He used as an example a contrast between Burke's description of the Queen of France, and Jeremy Taylor's of the dying Lady Carberry. 'While Burke speaks as an accomplished orator, Taylor touches the heights of Poetry' was Keble's conclusion. He asked if anyone could deny that the latter was 'the outpouring of a full heart?', while he held Burke's piece to be 'overcarefully framed to appeal to an audience'.[13]

Lecture IV made the distinction between Primary and Secondary poets clear. Primary poets were 'spontaneously moved by impulse' and the 'resort to composition for relief and solace of a burdened or overwrought mind'. Secondary poets were imitators, and more self-conscious poets: they copied the ideas and expressions of Primary Poets and were not honestly inspired. Keble named as a Secondary poet 'Dryden, (may I be forgiven for saying so)'[14]. He was making the point that a Primary poet had to be self-consistent, something which the political and religious trimmer Dryden could never be considered as. He settled Dryden's position on the Parnassian slopes with the sentence, 'One quality alone there is unworthy of a great poet: so wanting in self-consistency is he that we feel he never heartily and sincerely praised any human being, or felt any real enthusiasm for any subject he took up.'

It was absolutely necessary for a Primary poet to be

indifferent to novelty, and untainted by ambition. In a curious way, it is noticeable that Keble's conditions for a Primary poet coincided very much with his own precepts which governed the conduct of his own life. Keble shunned novelty and although quite obviously a very able man turned aside ambitious thoughts. He sought the ordinary life of a country parish rather than the distinctions which a purely academic life would have offered him. In retiring from the election for Provost of Oriel, leaving the field to Hawkins, and in emulating the example of George Herbert's ideal country parson, it was almost as though Keble was keenly following an inverted ambition: as if following it, he knew he was doing better in the sight of God than other men of his ability in more public ways. Perhaps there was almost a degree of inverted pride in endeavouring to humble himself: certainly he knew there was virtue in his choice: it accorded with the rules of asceticism and came close to his revered George Herbert's conception of the parson's life. Newman has written a valuable description of Keble which appeared as a prefatory letter at the beginning of the collected *Occasional Papers and Reviews*. Keble's positive desire for the unsensational, almost for obscurity, was shown in that letter by Newman's story of Keble's comment on a friend's sermon, which has already been referred to (p. 37). The friend had preached the sermon before the University and Keble had asked to borrow it for he had heard it praised. When Keble had read it, he handed it back and whispered in his friend's ear, 'Don't be original'. The remark was characteristic of both the restraint and the conservatism which showed itself in every aspect of Keble's life, whether religious, literary or political.

So it was necessary to test a Primary poet on his degree of striving after originality: '... let us apply also the test which is based on his pride in, or indifference to, a reputation for originality, as well as the previous test of consistency.' It was for this sin of pride that Keble condemned Young's 'Night Thoughts': he wrote of Young as one of '... those who nervously strain after something wholly new or unheard of, and even at their best, certainly evince their ambition but not the simplicity of truth'.[15]

Keble went on to lay down that the Primary poet 'must not overshoot the mark'; he had to observe a due reserve. The close relationship between Religion and Poetry was marked by this common respect for the qualities of reserve; and as in Religion, so in Poetry, there is naturally a certain mystic leaning. Keble expatiated on reserve: he mentioned the 'modest reticence' observable in Pindar, and quoted the Early Church Fathers who insisted that care should be taken 'lest opponents and mockers should attain knowledge of sacramental mysteries and the key-words of faith'. In the Church, only those initiated by confirmation are permitted to partake of the holiest mystery, and Keble saw that Divine Poetry demanded similar conditions of initiation. Primary poets were like the priests of Religion and had to be noted for their moderation and reserve, '... the more keenly a man pursues any desired object, the less inclined he is, for the most part, to discourse of it to all and sundry'.[16]

This led Keble into a discussion of the connection between Poetry and Irony. George Saintsbury commented, on this particular part of Keble's lectures, that it was one of the most interesting, at the same time as he commended Keble's brilliant *aperçus* 'on different poets ancient and modern'.[17]

Keble observed that Primary poets made frequent and innocent use of irony. They often drew a veil over their most intense emotions, but it was a veil which those who knew how to look could see through. Keble showed how Spenser in 'Epithalamion' and in 'The Faerie Queene' betrayed what was really in his mind, 'without alienating the sympathy of his readers, or betraying his secret passion, he could ease his own love troubles through poetic expression'.[18]

And Keble saw the importance of revision for a poet in his work: the intense outpourings of a poet's soul had to be looked over, time and again:

> What is more common than for men who have been under some strong emotion to feel impelled to read over and over again what they may chance to have written at the moment: to linger over almost every word; to erase, to add, to recast the whole: and hardly to please themselves with any form?

Revision was to be expected, and, in the end, the Primary poet would produce 'as many kinds of poems as there are emotions of the human mind'.[19]

Keble realised that, on occasions, the poet was as though in a mad frenzy, and his poetry acted as a relief to that madness in his mind. Reluctant to make known openly and publicly his innermost, powerful feelings, the poet took recourse to expressing them under the veil of poetry, thus curing himself of his mania which otherwise would have brought about the disintegration of his mind. There is obvious in this way of thinking the underlying idea of the act of confession as a means of rescuing the mind from despair and ruin; but to confess publicly would be unbearable. Similarly, in Keble's theories can be seen ideas which promise what was to come from the thoughts of Freud. Although he was unaware of the fact, Keble was touching on the means of healing the sick and obsessed minds, not only of poets, but ordinary people too. M.H. Abrams has commented:

> It may seem odd that this radical, proto-Freudian theory, which conceives literature as distinguished wish-fulfillment, serving the artist as a way back from incipient neurosis, should come out of the doubly conservative environment of High-Anglicanism and the Oxford Chair of Poetry.[20]

In the review of the *Life of Sir Walter Scott,* Keble was explicit: he went so far as to state that poetry existed as a kind of safety valve which tended to preserve poets from mental disease. He showed how some critics thought that poetry was allied to extravagance and distraction of mind, and referred to Plato as saying that poetry lay in an enthusiasm which to men appeared like insanity. Aristotle, too, thought that a poet should be possessed with some overpowering emotion which required such relief that would prevent it from terminating in madness.[21] At this point, Keble mentioned Dryden again, saying that although he had versatility, he was lacking enthusiasm or passionate devotion; and Dryden was placed very firmly in the second category of poets.

Maybe Dryden was too sane to have been a Primary poet. Certainly Lucretius, whom Keble just managed to concede a place on the edge of the first class of poets, was touched by mental disease. Keble showed how Lucretius had a passion for limitless space, and commented: 'Undoubtedly the study of the more abstruse regions of philosophy, which we now call Metaphysics, and wherein Lucretius took special delight, always seems to have included an element not very much removed from a sort of insanity.'[22]

If you contemplated infinity, you were mad; and, in turn, minds disordered were given to prophecy. Such was the nature of the Primary poet: he had elements of mystical meditation, and prophetic utterance about him: all of which added up to madness.

Since his Lectures were very largely based on his reading of the Classical poets, Keble's examples and illustrations were from those authors. Primary poets were rare; and Keble limited them properly to Homer, Aeschylus, Pindar and Virgil. These four belonged to the great tradition: Euripides and Lucretius were considered as just belonging on the periphery of Primary rank, but they had serious and limiting faults. Sophocles failed the test of Primary poet, 'so far, at all events, as concerns that domain of Poetry which touches men's feelings and emotions'.[23] In Lecture XXVIII, Keble dealt with Sophocles, and wrote that '... although a careful student of Sophocles, I have not been able to trace any one deep feeling and pervading passion running through the whole of his work. Thus I am doubtful whether anything of the sort possessed him.' There was too much artifice in Sophocles, and no trace of humour; and humour was necessary in tragedy, which Keble regarded highly, as 'the most grave and austere order of poetry'.[24] This must have been so, in Keble's mind, because of the great purging of serious emotions that takes place in the spectator's soul, as well as that sort of catharsis which must have happened in the poet's soul when he wrote his tragic poetry.

Certainly the tragic and epic poets ranked higher in Keble's preference than lyric poets. The distinction was only too clear, and was one of sincerity and sustained feeling. It was far easier for lyric poets to affect being other than what they really were. Artifice was more in evidence: like Sophocles, lyric poets were inclined to be a poet made, not a poet born.[25] Keble wrote: 'It is far more easy to pretend to feel a strong emotion in a short poem, and the result is more convincing: while it is hardly possible for anyone to use borrowed notes in a long epic or tragic story.'[26]

It is, however, more interesting to read Keble's opinions of English poets, and to receive those *aperçus* which Saintsbury talked of. In this way, from Keble's analyses and judgements of the sort of poetry others wrote, it is possible to add other dimensions to his theory of poetry, and possible to relate his opinions to his own poetry.

Shakespeare, the great tragic, poetic dramatist ranked among the Primary English poets. Shakespeare, who was following received traditions, wrote often in the tragic vein: for Keble, *Hamlet* was 'the noblest and greatest of all the tragedies'; and Shakespeare observed a strict reverence for the presentation of ghosts. His ghosts, Keble thought, were always the agents of moral good: they were divine messengers who spoke what God intended.[27]

Next to Shakespeare, the other English poets, who were not contemporaries, whom Keble especially admired were Spenser, Herbert and Milton. Spenser he compared, in a way, with Virgil. He thought it curious that, like Virgil, Spenser could compose at the wish of a patron. But, he explained, the genuine poet does not object to far-fetched subjects: indeed, he often prefers them, 'so long only as some secret path is open, whereby it may quietly digress to the themes it naturally delights in and holds dear'. As Virgil was able to write at the suggestion of Augustus, so Spenser could compose prompted by others. And often some trifling subject would cloak some hidden, important meaning. Spenser wrote on a fly caught in a spider's web, 'Muiopotmos'; Pope, 'on a stolen tress of a lady's hair'.[28]

Earlier in the Lectures, Keble had already stated that the veil of allegory allows the writer to say what he would not say publicly: it enabled Spenser to describe intimately woes and sorrows of the noble family of the Sidneys through Thestylis. At this point, Keble went on to reflect the ideas of Wordsworth:

> ... and more important still, the device enables the poet to introduce in support of the feeling which he is portraying, those objects in which all poets are wont, and rightly wont, to take eminent delight, woods, mountains and trees, in short, all that belongs to the country and rural life.[29]

Such was the case with Milton, too: and here Keble quoted the example of 'Lycidas'. The poet's inmost thoughts, enthusiasms, and emotions were protected from being exposed to the 'full blaze of daylight'. Herbert exemplified the technique as well. Keble praised the 'tact and judgement of the writers, in choosing subjects remote from those which in truth hold their affection'. So, Herbert hid his deep love of God, which utterly consumed him, behind a cloud of precious conceits; and Keble thought that 'the result appears to most readers inappropriate, not to say chilling and repellent'.[30] Keble excused Herbert, as he had excused the Elizabethans, by the prevalent tone and taste of the age. Nevertheless, what was admirable, was 'Herbert's modest reserve which made him veil under these refinements his deep piety'.

Milton must have posed a great problem for Keble's critical judgement, as he has for many more eminent literary critics. Cromwell's secretary was certainly not the man to whom Keble's sympathies could immediately go out. Indeed, in 'Sacred Poetry',[31] Keble censured Milton: he said that Milton's fault was intellectual pride, and his generation's spiritual pride. Earlier, in the same review, he said that Spenser always made vice contemptible or odious, Milton looked on vice as a judge, and Shakespeare as a satirist. Despite Milton's intellectual pride, and his Puritanism, abhorrent to Keble, the Lectures referred to him as 'our learned poet Milton' who was compared with Homer.[32] Milton, who has caused so much schizophrenic judgement in critics, was given epic status and primary rank among poets.

Of Keble's contemporaries, apart from Wordsworth, it was Sir Walter Scott who was the most important poet for Keble. In the review of the *Life of Sir Walter Scott,*[33] Keble wrote, 'Scott at least must be set down as a Primary Poet in every sense of the word.' This was a marvellous, and enviable, accolade for Scott, but then, according to Keble, he had the ruling passion of the spirit of Border chivalry, and the ability to turn all to its purpose, at the same time as veiling his tastes from unsympathetic minds. In addition, although Scott's poetry has not withstood the test of time, Keble thought that, 'Every year proves more decidedly that his popularity was not of the flighty and ephemeral kind.' It was regrettable that Scott should have given up poetry, because he considered Byron better. Keble wondered what Scott's influence would have been if he had become the Poet of the Church, which was, of course, what Keble had become. In Scott there was the love of the marvellous and the supernatural, a consciousness of faith acting within him, and an inclination to the old Catholic Church. Keble postulated that so far as Scott was concerned, 'The tenets of the presence of good and evil angels, of the power of the sacramentals ... unencumbered of Romanism ... would have found ready entrance into a willing mind.'[34] Scott had a known preference in religious song for the 'Stabat Mater' and 'Dies Irae'. He had translated the 'Dies Irae'. and Keble detected in Scott what he described as similar to Burke's 'reachings and graspings'.[35]

In the Lectures, Scott is referred to as the 'noblest of all poets in our own day'[36] and 'one whom I can never mention without reverence'. Previously in Lecture IX, Scott had been compared with Homer, 'By no poet, in my judgement, has that vivacious, swift, Homeric rush been more nearly approached'; and Keble went on to say, 'Homer saw before his eyes what he described ... Scott had the harder task, to reclaim from oblivion and obscurity, as best he could, a type and order of men long since departed.'[37] Not content with the fair comparison with Homer, later in Lecture XXVI, Scott was compared with one of the great Classical, Primary poets, Pindar. Keble even called Scott the 'Scotch Pindar'.[38] Scott took his inspiration from mountains and country life, in which he saw memories of past heroes belonging to a fierce, indomitable clan. Likewise, from country life and the beauties of Nature, Pindar, the lover of flowers, had drawn his inspiration.

When, however, Keble considered other contemporary poets such as Bryon and Burns, it was clear that the idea of self-consistency played an important part in his evaluation. The poet had to represent in his own life the power and position of moral good: otherwise his poetry lacked any degree of high moral seriousness. Byron approached the heights of Parnassus in Keble's judgement, but, in the end, had to be condemned to the lower plains. Byron grew unrestrained, arrogant and lacked reserve:

Popular favour has placed easily first among all poets of our time a man whom I too should rank high, had he not sullied his splendid powers by many serious vices, inexcusable in anyone, to say nothing of a great poet. Nothing if I may speak freely, has more powerfully contributed to his popular success than his lavish profusion and impetuous style in utter disregard whether what he writes be fit or becoming or not. This want of true modesty ...[39]

So far as primary rank was concerned, Byron forfeited all claim to a place in it. Keble stressed that it was 'essential to give utterance sparingly and only under veils and disguises, to the deepest feelings'.

Keble's conclusion about Byron at this point came in Lecture XIII, after Keble had spent some time arguing that a revolutionary spirit and democracy were both unsuitable for the inspiration of great poetry. It laid Keble open to the charge that you could not be a poet of any worth unless you were a Tory: indeed Keble regarded Homer as a Tory. And there is some truth in the charge. He wrote 'not only Homer but all true poets naturally incline to that party in a State which holds it a sacrilege to disturb what is peaceful, or to try to upset in mere pursuit of novelty practices sanctioned by ancient usage and religion'.[40] Keble held that in a democratic state 'the sole distinction will be that of wealth',[41] And he continued to say that 'once the revolutionary and mercenary passion prevails, whether it be with individuals or communities, forthwith a certain unreasoning contempt for poetry possesses them'.

Such a poet was Byron, whose poetry did not exhibit that essential feature of due reserve, and did not observe reverence. It was all the more creditable to Scott that, at a time when the fortunes of his own political party were waning, he managed to keep out any resentment or bitterness from his poetry: indeed, any reference at all.[42]

But Byron was not dismissed easily. Keble returned to his admonition in Lecture XXXIV, where he wrote of Byron:

We have not yet, I apprehend, forgotten a poet, at once of noble birth and noble genius, who in our youth was held to have borne the palm of poetic art and power from nearly all his rivals. Ardent and profound as his poetic gift was, he spoilt it all by associating it with the wild dreams of those who, whether or not they really believe that either no Supreme Power or, if any, a Malignant Power, rules the universe, at any rate wish that it were so.[43]

It was this censure which led Keble on to condemn Shelley too; and it may be well to regard Keble's poem in *The Christian Year*, written for Palm Sunday, as a direct reference and prayer for these two lost souls. Walter Lock suggested the connection. Of Shelley, Keble wrote:

Another followed after him [Byron] ... but in command of language and of rhythm an even greater master, and as it would seem, of far more sensitive temperament. But it was fancied, with some probability, that even he was scarcely master of himself. In short they were, and are now, both of them, considered rather as unhappy than as impious.[44]

This judgement was either charitable or condescending; but Keble's poem had made the prayer that those whose hearts beat 'with the pulse of Poesy' might recognise and know that the gift was divine, and therefore not neglect their duty to God:

> He hath chosen you to lead
>   His Hosannas here below; —
> Mount, and claim your glorious meed;
>   Linger not with sin and woe.

Whether or not the prayer was heard by God, it was not heard by Byron or Shelley. In direct contrast to Keble's hero, Scott, whose lameness stimulated him to 'generous exertion', Keble wrote in the review of the *Life of Sir Walter Scott*,[45] Byron's lameness stimulated him to spleen: it was a 'thorn in the side of that inordinate vanity'.

Of other contemporaries, Southey was dismissed for seeking after novelty. In Lecture XXXIII Keble classed him with modern poets who thought that they achieved nothing unless they produced some fact which nobody had heard of before, but which their own eyes had witnessed. Keble alluded to Southey's 'Curse of Kehama' in the following deprecating sentence:

> Hence we have those far-fetched stories, now from the Indies, now from the remotest West, such as a description of an Indian fig-tree, or of American birds, or whatever else reading of many books may have particularly impressed on learned men.[46]

Finally, very different from Southey's undignified search for novelty, was Burns's poetry. In a way he resembled Byron. Burns had, in Keble's view, great qualities which took him near the company of the Primary poets. In Lecture II Burns had the honour of being translated into Greek when his similarities to Theocritus were being discussed.[47] The lines 'I look to the West when I gae to rest' breathed the very spirit of Theocritus, so that Keble thought them more sweetly expressed in Greek. Later in the fourteenth lecture, Keble compared Burns with Homer. Burns resembled Homer 'in his passionate love both of rustic pleasures and wild scenery, and also, I think, in his poverty'.[48] It was the poverty which Burns had to endure, and disliked so much, which embittered him, so greatly, against the rich and fortunate on whom Homer, by contrast, looked with sweet and kindly temper. Like Byron, Burns fell into evil ways:

> But in this respect, as throughout life, a mad and truly reckless craving for pleasure proved the greatest curse to him. Hence sprang all his angry feelings, his anxiety, his restlessness: hence a self-accusing conscience, unable to view either man or nature: hence his blind railing against the powers that be.[49]

In spite of Burns's early reading of other poets, and his learning from them, there was a surprisingly unequal and inconsistent quality about his work. Keble considered 'The Cotter's Saturday Night' a most beautiful poem:

> See him preparing for his Sabbath with the family Bible at his side: what a glimpse we have not only of the place

of home but of deep piety. Will anyone deny that the tone of these lines is not only charming and delightful, but even reverent and religious? Who does not lament and marvel, too, that the man who wrote it could so rapidly have declined to sottish courses and indulged in ribald abuse, pleasures in which, if ever man did, he revelled keenly and eagerly?[50]

As with Byron, Burns's way of life was inconsistent: it lacked a permanent tenor of reverence and reserve. One quality alone was constant, and that lay in his feeling for beauty, which in turn was reflected in his poetry. This constant vein of feeling was 'always guiding in one direction a mind which, apart from this, seems so inconsistent'.

In his last lecture, Keble admitted his inadequacy. He had failed to define Poetry: he had met with the same failure that every other critic has ecnountered who has tried the same task. Yet in this limited sense, if Keble's forty lectures were a failure, they were a splendid and interesting failure; and they represent the largest part of his literary struggle to define his theories about poetry. His two classes of poet, the Primary — inspired, original, driven by impulse, consistent, reverent, reserved, religious in the sense of awe and admiration that Nature, or God through Nature, is regarded — and the Secondary — the imitators and the artificial — Keble made perfectly clear, and by example he illustrated and enforced his arguments. By his own critical lights, Keble himself ought to rank with the Primary poets, and perhaps it is only because we are the inheritors of a democratic society conceived in the age of liberal reform that we can no longer judge the true worth of his poetry. Poetry, which he saw beginning to lie dishonoured and neglected in his own time, perhaps, in his sense, is thoroughly disregarded. In a democracy, where wealth is the only distinction, what chance have the Muses, '...they cannot help a man to make or keep a fortune'.[51]

Although Keble's ideas about poetry were notable and clearly argued, he realised his own sense of failure, and expressed it with his characteristic modesty: 'I see how that I have only been a worker in a small corner of a very wide territory, and that I have not explained what Poetry is in itself, but rather have pointed to certain sure marks and attributes of it.'[52]

Such a sentence, full of Keble's humility, states well the reason why Keble's theory of poetry has been overlooked. A combination of Keble's own reserve, his shunning of publicity, the fact that he was first a theologian, and that the lectures were published in Latin, tended to obscure what he had to say from a wide critical audience. In fact, Keble was not so isolated as he would at first appear. He showed the interdependence of art, in his case poetry, and the age in which it is created: he saw it as important. It became, of course, almost a Victorian ideal; and it becomes clear that Keble, at the same time as anticipating part of what Freud had to say, also preceded, in this respect, Arnold and Ruskin.

Professor Keble, as a literary critic, was more important in the nurturing of nineteenth-century criticism, than his neglect has given cause to show.

NOTES

1. *Occ. Papers and Reviews*, p.91.
2. 'Poetry is divinely inspired'.
3. *Lectures*, Vol. II, p.483.
4. *Lectures*, Vol. II, p.473.
5. *Lectures*, Vol. II, p.479.
6. *Lectures*, Vol. I, pp.70-1.
7. *Lectures*, Vol. I, p.71.
8. *Lectures*, Vol. II, p.482.
9. *Lectures*, Vol. II, p.219.
10. *Lectures*, Vol. I, p.22.
11. *Lectures*, Vol. II, p.35.
12. *Lectures*, Vol. II, p.368.
13. *Lectures*, Vol. I, p.50.
14. *Lectures*, Vol. I, p.71.
15. *Lectures*, Vol. I, p.72.
16. *Lectures*, Vol. I, p.76.
17. *Lectures*, Vol. I, Translator's note, p.5.
18. *Lectures*, Vol. I, p.82.
19. *Lectures*, Vol. I, p.88.
20. M.H. Abrams, *The Mirror and the Lamp*, (Norton Library) Oxford, 1958, p.147.
21. *Occ. Papers and Reviews*, p.21.
22. *Lectures*, Vol. II, pp.344-5.
23. *Lectures*, Vol. II, p.206.
24. *Lectures*, Vol. I., p.328.
25. *Lectures*, Vol. II, p.223.
26. *Lectures*, Vol. II, p.96.
27. *Lectures*, Vol. II, p.25.

28. *Lectures*, Vol. II, p.377.
29. *Lectures*, Vol. II, p.98.
30. *Lectures*, Vol. II, p.99.
31. *Occ. Papers and Reviews*, p.103.
32. *Lectures*, Vol. I, p.263.
33. *Occ. Papers and Reviews*, p.66.
34. *Occ. Papers and Reviews*, p.76.
35. *Occ. Papers and Reviews*, p.77.
36. *Lectures*, Vol. II, p.148.
37. *Lectures*, Vol. I, p.148.
38. *Lectures*, Vol. II, p.168.
39. *Lectures*, Vol. I, p.258.
40. *Lectures*, Vol. I, p.256.
41. *Lectures*, Vol. I, p.257.
42. *Lectures*, Vol. II, p.162.
43. *Lectures*, Vol. II, p.338.
44. *Lectures*, Vol. II, p.339.
45. *Occ. Papers and Reviews*, Oxford, 1877, p.51.
46. *Lectures*, Vol. II, pp.312-13.
47. M.H. Abrams, *The Mirror and the Lamp*, Oxford, 1958, p.144, comments that the lectures' 'somewhat bravura quality is emphasised by the lecturer's device of setting off a lyric of Robert Burns from its Latin context by translating it into Theocritan Greek'.
48. *Lectures*, Vol. I, p.276.
49. *Lectures*, Vol. I, pp.276-7.
50. *Lectures*, Vol. II, p.95.
51. *Lectures*, Vol. I, p.257.
52. *Lectures*, Vol. II, p.465.

PART III

John Keble's Poetry

CHAPTER 6

The Christian Year:
Background and Reputation

Now that the basic principles of both Keble's religious thought and his aesthetic theories have been determined, it is necessary to examine their relationship to his poetry and **the** sort of poetry he wrote.

Writing in 1866, J.C. Shairp, Professor of Humanity in the University of St Andrew, extolled the virtue of the English public school education for most boys; but he had qualifications:

> ... but for natures of finer texture, for all boys who have a decided and original bias, how much is there that the rough handling of a public school would ruthlessly crush? From all the better public schools coarse bullying, we know, has disappeared; but for peculiarity of any kind, for whatever does not conform itself to the 'tyrant tradition' — a manly and straightforward one we admit — they have but little tolerance. If Keble had once imbibed the public school spirit, *The Christian Year* would either never have been written, or it would have lacked some of its tenderest, most characteristic traits.[1]

Apart from the interesting sidelight which the passage gives on the Victorian public school, it is important to note that Keble's isolation from other children, apart from his own family, in the Gloucestershire countryside, made him what he was. According to Shairp if Keble's character had been roughened by contact with the world, his poetry would have lacked much of what constituted its appeal.

From his father's house at Fairford, Keble proceeded in 1807 at the age of fifteen, to Corpus Christi College, Oxford. There,

108

too, he was somewhat isolated, although to a lesser degree, surrounded by a close coterie of friends. It was undoubtedly this upbringing which made him so intimate with his brother and sisters, and which makes his letters therefore of detailed interest.

Before the publication of *The Christian Year* in 1827, Keble had been composing and collecting his poems, showing them or reading them to friends or relations. His letters to Thomas show his liking for the occasional doggerel rhyme: in fact, one letter written on 23 January 1812 is wholly a rhyming one:

> Tell Jones to bring up my penknife when he comes —
>   I don't think I have got any
> More news, nor any [illegible], but don't forget my botany.
> My love to all the world — If the word rebel was but spelt
>   reebel.
> I shouldn't have so much trouble in finding a rhyme to this —
>   I am yrs,
>
> > John Keble.[2]

Later, in May 1828, he included a simple verse for Sarah, Thomas's daughter, whom he nicknamed Pussy:

> ... but the poachers have cut off Mr Blackwell's peacock's head. This seems to be all the news I can remember just now: so I must go on with sentiment. Have you got any pinks out? we have plenty: and one jolly thrush which has only opened his mouth of late. Pussy here's a song for you: 'I'll sing a song for pussy [*sic*] / a nosegay in her hand / four and twenty spring flowers / tied in a band / and when the May winds whistled / the pinks began to smell / and wasn't that a posy sweet / to please my Lady well.'[3]

Again, in 1829, an undated letter to Thomas shows his commenting on the political situation of the day and rounding off with a rhyming couplet:

> So what with this, and what with that
> There's hardly known what is what.

His serious poetry, however, was not given to such trivial usage, and in any case it was a much more private and personal affair according with his views on poetry, and with his religious belief, as already discussed. It was with great reluctance that he published *The Christian Year,* in 1827, and his final decision to do so was largely due to the persuasion of his father, and his friends, especially John Davison, one of his Oriel College close companions. H.P. Liddon quoted Pusey as saying: 'He [Keble] published *The Christian Year* while Newman was just emerging from Evangelicalism and I was busy with Arabic, in the hope of counter-working, with God's help, German rationalism on the Old Testament.'[4]

It is doubtful whether Keble had Pusey's hope in mind; at this stage it was more likely that Pusey was attributing his own hope to Keble's motives for publishing. Keble's ambitions were much more modest and he veiled his identity beneath anonymity; and his anxiety about the publication was very real. He confided to Isaac Williams, another poet of the Oxford Movement, that the volume of poems would fail: 'It will be still-born, I know very well, but it is only in obedience to my father's wishes that I publish it, and that is some comfort.'[5]

In the event, Keble's fears were unjustified. *The Christian Year* had one of the best publication records in the nineteenth century. J.S. Rowntree, in a contribution to *The Friends' Quarterly Examiner,*[6] pointed out that *The Christian Year* achieved an average annual publication of 10,000 copies during the first fifty years after its appearance, and stressed that it must have circulated in the homes of Low Churchmen as well as High Churchmen, of Unitarians as well as Roman Catholics: it brought through its reading and meditation, through devotional study and contemplation, a measure of consolation to all kinds of people. Certainly for Anglicans, next to the Bible and the Prayer Book, it occupied a place of familiar importance, whose source of spiritual comfort was to be equalled only later on, by 'In Memoriam'. It was, in fact, a Victorian best seller.

M. Mare and A.C. Percival described[7] how all of C.M. Yonge's well-educated characters have thoroughly read and digested the poems, 'Even the profane Owen, in *Hopes and Fears,* can come out with an apposite quotation, likening the green and white of a girl's party dress to the snowdrop of one of the poems.' The poem in question is the one for Tuesday of Easter Week, and is one of the few poems which has a title, 'To the Snow-drop':

> Thou first-born of the year's delight,
>   Pride of the dewy glade,
> In vernal green and virgin white,
>   Thy vestal robes array'd.

Both the poem and the 'profane Owen' episode show well the influence of Wordsworth, and in particular to his 'Immortality Ode', which produced what now appears to have been a cult for moralising over natural beauty.

Yet it is not only Yonge's novels which show the popularity of *The Christian Year* (she was after all a close friend and great admirer of Keble), but others do as well. Miss Fontover in Hardy's *Jude the Obscure*, 'wore a cross and beads round her neck as her only ornament, and knew the *Christian Year* by heart'. Maggie Tulliver read *The Christian Year:* 'She read so eagerly and constantly in her three books, the Bible, Thomas a Kempis, and *The Christian Year* (no longer rejected as a "hymn-book") that they filled her mind with a continual stream of rhythmic memories.'[8] And Arthur Pendennis remembered reading it with his mother.

Such was the popularity of *The Christian Year* that Bishop Westcott made the extravagant claim that a verse of Keble was worth volumes of Tennyson. J.C. Shairp wrote that the Oxford Movement bequeathed '... two permanent monuments of genius' to the Church of England, Newman's sermons and *The Christian Year*'.

In his 'Notes on *The Christian Year*', J.S. Rowntree prophesied that examination papers of the future would ask candidates to name ten of the foremost British authors who flourished in the nineteenth century and the works for which they are famed. He thought that:

> All present indication point to *The Christian Year* as one
> of the few books written in the nineteenth century that
> may be widely read in the twentieth century,
> and that John Keble will be one of the ten authors named

by those who obtain the highest number of marks for their answers to our hypothetical question.

Rowntree was wrong in his estimation of Keble and in his prediction; and Owen Chadwick commented in his book *The Mind of the Oxford Movement:*

> I confess that I can only understand, with a bare assent of the intellect, the influence exerted by *The Christian Year*. Keble has moments of grandeur, moments of deep sincerity and simplicity; but the moments of bathos or superficiality, bring you down again to the dust too soon after you have soared above it. To read *The Christian Year* feels like seeing an honest and moral play where the illusion is often being broken. I give this only as a reflection of personal taste. Perhaps there are men who can still, like their forefathers, elevate *The Christian Year* to the level of *Pilgrim's Progress* or *The Imitation of Christ*.[9]

Nevertheless, during the nineteenth century the public took readily and naturally to *The Christian Year* during the various phases of its numerous editions. Parker and Company, the publisher, authorised the following summary which is printed in Keble's *Occasional Papers and Reviews:* it shows the number of editions and copies issued, from *The Christian Year's* first publication until the expiration of the copyright in 1873:

The Christian Year Summary

	Eds	Total Copies
From 1827 to end of 1837	16	26,500
From 1838 to end of 1847	14	39,000
From 1848 to end of 1857	19	63,000
From 1858 to end of 1867	60	119,500
from 1868 to April, 1873	31	57,500
Total	140	305,500

After copyright expired many editions came into the market, and numbers are difficult to ascertain. It is known, however, that between April 1873 and December 1875, Parkers issued at reduced prices upwards of 70,000 copies. Of the first ten years' 26,500 copies, the first edition was issued in July 1827 and numbered 500 copies; the second edition issued around November 1827 numbered 750 copies. It is this second one that Keble wrote to Thomas about on 30 October 1827. In the letter he mentioned that Hurrell Froude was his proof reader:

> I hear from Oxford that ye book is just beginning to be reprinted, and I have made some few and slight alterations, but things won't come when I ask for them — they are just like John Simmons. Froude is my corrector of the press: but he is very unhappy at having to teach what he doesn't understand himself: but I am going to comfort him with the example of his betters.[10]

The third edition, issued around March 1826, numbered 1,250 copies. Of the 119,500 copies issued in the nine years 1857-67, there were forty-six editions between 1858 and April 1866 (Keble died on 29 March 1866) which comprised 97,500 copies; and between May 1866 and December 1867, there were fourteen editions which totalled 22,000 copies. By any standards in the history of books, the achievement of ninety-five editions during the space of the author's lifetime, and one hundred and forty editions before copyright ran out, is a remarkable one.

Keble always cast a careful, critical eye over the proofs, and editions as they came out; but he did not just leave it at that. His friends helped to keep the strain pure as well. In a letter to his brother, dated 25 September 1839, as well as reporting the intimate detail that, 'Charlotte had her ears syringed today by Mr Sainsbury of Romsey', Keble went on: 'The little Psalter is come, did I tell you, and another Edition of the Xtian Year wanted, so if you know of any errata in the latter it will be a charity to send them.'[11]

So far as it is possible to find out from Thomas's letters he did not find any errata; but he may have passed some on by word of mouth.

A measure of *The Christian Year's* immense success and popularity can be judged from the Introduction of G.W. Doane's American first edition. Signed on 1 July 1834, the introduction tells that Doane came across 'Holy Baptism' accidentally: her ordered a copy of *The Christian Year* from his bookseller: 'The book when received, was read with unmingled delight; and no volume of inspired poetry has ever given him such rich and continual satisfaction.' Doane continued, referring to himself, the editor, objectively: 'From the time of its first reading, the Editor has never ceased to recommend it to his personal friends; and in 'The Banner of the Church' and in other ways, to call the public attention to its merits.'[12]

In its own way, too, Doane's introduction might provide some evidence of how the popularity of *The Christian Year* was boosted by other clergymen: if he were typical, the book's recommendations would have been many and influential. No doubt the clergy did find in it a suitable companion piece to the Prayer Book, as Keble wanted, and undoubtedly they publicised it before their congregations, and approved of it in their parish magazines. The historian, G. Kitson Clark,[13] argues that the standard of church-going was high. The religious census of 1851, although a much suspected and debated investigation and report, on Sunday 30 March of that year, counted the worshippers at each of the services, morning, afternoon and evening: whoever was in charge of the service took the count, if he were willing to do so, in every church or chapel in the land. The final figure for the people who had attended some service or other, was 7,261,032. It was supposedly estimated, making allowances for those people who attended twice or three times, and for those who for good reason (sickness or old age) could not attend. The figure, which is one for England and Wales, should be considered in relation to the total population which was 17,927,609 produced by the 1851 census. The census can be attacked because of its estimated uncertainties, but, nevertheless, it is not difficult to understand how *The Christian Year*, assiduously publicised, and at the same time hitting the appropriate key of comforting sentiment, sold a total of 305,500 copies between 1827 and 1873 to its devotees.

It is important to note, at this point, in considering the background of *The Christian Year*, a little about Keble's character, because it seems, at times, that the tone and sentiment of his poetry could belie his own behaviour: it is sometimes difficult to reconcile the poet's kindliness and ministering humility with some of his actions which would seem uncharitable in the extreme unless his integrity and sincerity were obvious. For instance, Geoffrey Faber recorded in *Oxford Apostles* the incident involving Keble and Grenfell, one of Arnold's masters at Rugby.[14] Grenfell had travelled to Oxford in order to vote against the proposal, supported by Keble, to deprive Dr Hampden of his vote for the Select Preachers: the High Churchmen considered Hampden heretical. After the vote had been taken Grenfell saw Keble in the High Street, on the other side of the road, and crossed so that he might shake Keble's hand. Keble, however, held his hand out of reach, and said solemnly. 'Grenfell! You have sacrificed at the altar of Jupiter, and I renounce your friendship from this day.' Curiously enough, Thomas Arnold took up Keble's figure of speech, perhaps intentionally, some time later when writing to Sir John Coleridge about Keble in 1841: 'Now that I do not believe in it [Keble's Holy Catholic Church] in Keble's sense is most true; I would just as soon worship Jupiter; and Jupiter's idolatry is scarcely farther from Christianity in my judgment, than the idolatry of the priesthood.' No doubt Grenfell's story had made its way back to Rugby and Arnold, and, as a reflection on Arnold himself, it would have somewhat annoyed him.

Arnold, as early as 1823, had been a critic in praise of Keble's poems: he had written

It is my firm opinion that nothing equal to them exists in our language: the wonderful knowledge of Scripture, the purity of heart, and the richness of poetry, which they exhibit, I never saw paralleled.[15]

In a way, it was Arnold who set the tone for Keble's many admirers, eulogists and apologists who followed.

J.C. Shairp registers the most extravagant praise of Keble. He wrote of Keble's 'affectionate nature' expanding 'as a flower in the sun' in Oxford's surroundings: he continued, 'His affection toward the friends he made at Oxford was warm and deep, and lasted in most instances with his life.' At least Shairp had the conscience to make the qualification 'in most instances', although he did not amplify it. Shairp told of a brother scholar of Keble's at Corpus, who, when a fifty-five years' friendship came to an end, could say of him: 'It was the singular happiness of his nature, remarkable even in his undergraduate days, that love for him was always sanctified, as it were by reverence — reverence that did not make the love less tender, and love that did but add intensity to the reverence.'[16]

The answer to this apparent problem in the interpretation of Keble's character and, consequently, of some of his actions lies in Walter Lock's assertion that although Keble could be quick-tempered in reaction to what was said, and therefore often spoke sharply, he was always guarded and fair in what he wrote. Lock should have made the distinction between writing privately and publicly, for Keble's letters show that he could often be severe on people especially in a politically biased way. Local squires, such as Barker, who showed Whigish tendencies came in for heavy criticism when Keble wrote to Thomas. Similarly, on moral grounds, Keble could be spitefully eloquent to Thomas. In 1829 he wrote:

> We had a battle at Coln yesterday between one of those troublesome Jack Kibbles and another favourite of my father, Charles Knight. This is to illustrate ye good effects of the Beer River when it begins to run and all in spite of Sir R. Peel's very polite letter to Mr. Peters, in which he explains that the object of it is to prevent the immoral consumption of spirits.[17]

However, in public whether he was expressing himself in print, or whether he was preaching, Keble considered carefully what he had to say. Newman described Keble's style of delivering sermons. In the letter which prefaces Keble's *Occasional Papers and Reviews*, dated 29 October 1875, Newman wrote:

> I have too often heard him lecture, preach, and converse, not to have gained a habit of associating his matter and his diction with his living and breathing delivery. I have in my ears still the modulations and cadences of his voice, his pauses and emphatic points; I recollect what music there was in the simple earnestness and sweet gravity with which he spoke; the way he held his paper, his gestures,

his look, are all before me. I cannot judge even his style impartially; phrases and collocations of words, which others would call imperfections in his composition, are to me harmonized by the remembrance how he uttered them.

The fondness which Newman had for him, many others had as well. It was not only in his preaching that Keble's 'simple earnestness' and 'sweet gravity' were recollected: they were also appreciated in *The Christian Year.*

In the Postscript to Newman's prefatory letter,[18] Pusey quoted Sir John Coleridge, in a note, similarly writing about Keble's preaching:

> In delivery he did not give his sermons the advantage of an ordinarily eloquent preacher, but he was eminently winning: he let himself down, I do not mean in language or in argument, but in simplicity or childlike humility, to the most uneducated of his audience; he seemed always to account himself one of the sinners, one of the penitents, one even of the impenitents or careless, whom, he was addressing; and the very quietness, the almost tearful monotony of his delivery became extremely moving, when you recollected how learned, how able, how moved in his own heart, and how earnest was the preacher.

It was not only his closest friends, Newman and Pusey and Coleridge, who recognised Keble's qualities: it was the majority of people who did so, who had listened to him, or who had read his poems. Keble's modesty, his integrity, his 'sweet gravity' which produced, no doubt, the 'tearful monotony', his obvious sincerity and Christian conviction, all recommended themselves to his audience or his readers. No matter what sort of Christian his reader was, he could recognise these qualities in *The Christian Year:* the book was of great comfort and consolation. This accounted for its popularity and its reputation.

NOTES

1. J.C. Shairp, *John Keble,* Edinburgh, 1866, p.33.
2. Correspondence, C13.
3. Correspondence, C13.
4. H.P. Liddon, *Life of Pusey,* London, 1894, Vol. IV, p.340.
5. Quoted by Georgina Battiscombe in *John Keble,* London, 1963, p.104.
6. J.S. Rowntree, 'Notes on the Christian Year', *Friends Quarterly Examiner,* reprint, Bodleian Library, 1927.
7. M. Mare and A.C. Percival, *Victorian Best-Seller,* London, 1947.
8. George Eliot, *The Mill on the Floss,* London (Everyman), 1969, p.274.
9. Owen Chadwick, *The Mind of the Oxford Movement,* London, 1960, p.63.
10. Correspondence, C13.
11. Correspondence, C14.
12. *The Christian Year,* Philadelphia, 1834.
13. G. Kitson Clark, *The Making of Victorian England,* London, 1962.
14. Geoffrey Faber, *Oxford Apostles,* London, 1933.
15. Lock, p.54.
16. Shairp, p.37.
17. Correspondence, C13. Elsewhere Keble mentioned the Beer issue. A letter of 1832 reported: 'I have got one of our Beerhouses at Coln in a fair way of being trounced at last — but however I really believe the whole system is now going to be knocked on the head.' But it is clear from another extract that Thomas did not agree with him about the problem. In 1833 Keble wrote to Thomas: 'Did I tell you we had trounced Mr. Pope's beerhouse at Coln, and fined him 50 good shillings. Tho I dare say that you after your manner will think it a very improper interference.'
18. *Occ. Papers and Reviews,* p. xxi.

CHAPTER 7

The Christian Year
and Other Poetry

1 *Bishop Butler's Influence*

Typical of the poetry contained in *The Christian Year* is the poem written for the Sunday after Ascension. As with the majority of poems in *The Christian Year,* it has an epigraph: the poem is prefaced by a Biblical text. And indeed what the Biblical text is to a sermon, the epigraph is to one of Keble's poems. From it can be understood the theme and content of the poem: its words, more often than not, hold the clue to the poem's inspiration.

The epigraph, too, directs the way for those readers who might find the poems obscure. They become so much less obscure if the appropriate passage from the Bible is read, or if, as Keble hoped, the appropriate passage was already known. Yet again, however, the principle of economy, or reserve, operated in that a proper grasp of the poem might not be had unless the reader had been initiated into, and was educated in, the contents of the Bible.

The poem for the Sunday after Ascension has as its prefatory text: 'As every man hath received the gift, even so minister the same one to another, as good stewards of the manifold grace of God.' (St. Peter IV, 10)

The first three stanzas embrace much of what was Keble's purpose, and show many of his gifts:

> The Earth that in her genial breast
> Makes for the down a kindly nest,
> Where wafted by the warm south-west
> It floats at pleasure,
> Yields, thankful, of her very best,
> To nurse her treasure:

True to her trust, tree, herb, or reed,
She renders for each scatter'd seed,
And to her Lord with duteous heed
            Gives large increase:
Thus year by year she works unfeed,
            And will not cease.

Woe worth these barren hearts of ours,
Where Thou has set celestial flowers,
And water'd with more balmy showers
            Than e'er distill'd
In Eden, on th'ambrosial bowers —
            Yet nought we yield.[1]

In his Lectures Keble spoke of the divine nature of poetry and of it being the handmaid of religion: the close alliance between the two was of paramount importance and its expression is obvious here.

These stanzas show, too, the close connection between Nature and God, and stress that the creatures of God must pay due respect to their creator. The lesson is simple and straightforward, an enlargement of the Biblical text: whoever does not yield up to God what he should will invite the wrath of God.

The close relationship between 'the Earth', or Nature, and God in this poem and many of the others, is a sure mark of Wordsworth's influence. There is in the poems the constant idea that a scrutiny and contemplation of the objects of Nature inspire thoughts on the Divinity; by this scrutiny it easily becomes apparent that God reveals Himself to man through the objects of Nature; and from these thoughts a consequent moralising follows.

Undoubtedly the poem is significant in showing a direct relationship with what Keble admired in Wordsworth's poetic theories, and in Bishop Butler's philosophy. Dr Beek has written succinctly that 'Keble saw his fundamental religious principle, which was philosophically based on Butler's theory of analogy, confirmed by Wordsworth's poetic principle'.[2] A brief account of Butler's *The Analogy of Religion Natural and Revealed to the Constitution and Course of Nature* 1736 has already been given (see pp. 43-44) but Keble's acceptance of Butler's ideas and the way in which they influenced his poetry should be mentioned particularly here.

Butler taught that probability is the guide of life, and that our ordinary actions are not based on absolute certainty, but rather on a sense of what is probably true or likely to happen. In the case of death, Butler stated that in the analogy of nature there was no proof 'to afford us even the slightest presumption, that animals ever lose their living powers; much less, if it were possible, that they lose them by death: for we have no faculties wherewith to trace any beyond or through it, so as to see what becomes of them'.[3]

The *Analogy* was prescribed reading for students of theology both at Oxford and Cambridge in the nineteenth century so that it is not surprising that Keble was well read in Butler's views. As Newman wrote in his *Apologia,* Keble's difficulties over the philosophical principle of probability and the existence of God were met:

> ... by ascribing the firmness of assent which we [Roman Catholics] give to religious doctrine, not to the probabilities which introduce it, but to the living power of faith and love which accepts it. In matters of religion it is not merely probability which makes us intellectually certain, but probability as it is put to account by faith and love.[4]

In two particular ways Keble's poetry shows its debt to Bishop Butler. Butler's idea that man's state ia a dual one of sensation and of reflection had some bearing on Keble's thought; and considering Wordsworth's 'Lines written a few miles above Tintern Abbey' and the Preface to the *Lyrical Ballads*, it very likely influenced Wordsworth. Butler stated:

> When none of our senses are affected or appetites gratified, and yet we perceive and reason, and act; we may be said to exist or live in a state of reflection. Now it is by no means certain, that any thing which is dissolved by death, is any way necessary to the living being in this its state of reflection, after ideas are gained. For, though, from our present constitution and condition of being, our

external organs of sense are necessary for conveying in
ideas to our reflecting powers, as carriages, and levers, and
scaffolds in architecture: yet when these ideas are brought
in, we are capable of reflecting in the most intense degree,
and of enjoying the greatest pleasure, and feeling the
greatest pain, by means of that reflection, without any
assistance from our senses ...[5]

In this statement of Butler's philosophy there is distinct
similarity to Wordsworth's idea of 'recollection in tranquility'.

So, too, Keble's poetry, especially in *The Christian Year*,
shows the power of the state of reflection. Continually, the
Biblical text is pondered, and Keble's mind shifts to the objects
of Nature with which, by recourse to analogy, Keble often
amplifies what he is thinking. An example of this occurs in the
poem just quoted, in which the earth eventually yielding forth
harvest from the scattered seed stands, in contrast, as the
analogy for man's heart which on the whole yields badly to
God.

It is in this sense that Butler's philosophy, combined with
Wordsworth's influence on Keble, is most important to the
poetry.

Newman wrote in his *Apologia* that Butler's philosophy was
recast for him in *The Christian Year* by his new master, Keble.
From Butler, Keble learned that creation exists for man to
approach a close relationship with God. It is in Nature and her
objects that God partly reveals himself, which is the second
debt Keble's poetry owed especially to Butler. By implication,
whoever contemplates nature is likely to see, with greater
clarity, evidence of God. Moreover, in relation to the Scriptures,
Butler pointed out 'that he who believes the scripture to have
proceeded from him who is the Author of nature, may well
expect to find the same sort of difficulties in it, as are found in
the constitution of nature'.[6]

Wordsworth declared the stimulating power of concrete
objects rather than of abstractions in the Preface to the *Lyrical
Ballads,* and Keble continually had recourse to the objects of
Nature in his poetry in much the same way as Wordsworth. As
Prince writes in *Leading Ideas of Keble's* 'Christian Year', the
imagery of the poetry is that of the English countryside: he

mentions 'the wayside willow' which speaks of contentment, and:

> ... the dead leaves of the woodland are symbols of resignation; the strong clear note of the blackbird recalls all the words of friends that 'brace and cheer' us in times of sadness and depression; the glories of the autumn sunset are like the promise of the good man's joy in heaven; the flowers in their carelessness of fear, growing beneath our very foot-tread, are types of innocence.[7]

Prince draws attention to the line in Wordsworth's 'Ode to Duty', 'Flowers laugh before thee on their beds', and in doing so he underlines a marked similarity in the choice of imagery by Keble and Wordsworth. Clearly both do use the imagery of nature typical in the English countryside, hedges, flowers, violets and roses, hills and streams; and although Prince's interpretation of symbolism must be questioned in view of Tract 89, which is discussed later in this chapter, basically he is right in his analysis. Neither poet uses the imagery in any detailed way to give a picture of a particular place in any sense that might foreshadow the Pre-Raphaelites' realistic description of surroundings. The scenes, and especially Keble's, are of a general quality. Such, for example, is the scene in the second stanza of the poem for the Fifth Sunday after Easter:

> Deep is the silence as of summer noon,
>> When a soft shower
>> Will trickle soon,
> A gracious rain, freshening the weary bower —
>> O sweetly then far off is heard
>> The clear note of some lonely bird.

And the same is true of the second stanza of the poem for Monday in Whitsun-Week:

> Far opening down some woodland deep
> In their own quiet glade should sleep
>> The relics dear to thought,
> And wild-flower wreaths from side to side
> Their waving tracery hang, to hide
>> What ruthless Time has wrought.

> Their waving tracery hang, to hide
> What ruthless Time has wrought.

Of all the poems in *The Christian Year,* it is undoubtedly the ones written for Epiphany which show Keble's reliance on Nature, and his use of her examples for his Christian moralising. Perhaps it was these poems which Newman was thinking of particularly when he said that he saw so much of Bishop Butler's philosophy recast in *The Christian Year.* And, of course, it is suitable enough that these poems should have more to do with Nature than others, because the Epiphany Sundays fall in spring-time. The fourth and fifth stanzas of the poem for the first Sunday after Epiphany are a good example of Keble's moralising from the example of Nature:

> See the soft green willow springing
>   Where the waters gently pass,
> Every way her free arms flinging
>   O'er the moist and reedy grass.
> Long ere winter blasts are fled,
> See her tipp'd with vernal red,
> And her kindly flower display'd
> Ere her leaf can cast a shade.
>
> Though the rudest hand assail her,
>   Patiently she droops awhile,
> But when showers and breezes hail her,
>   Wears again her willing smile.
> Thus I learn Contentment's power
> From the slighted willow bower,
> Ready to give thanks and live
> On the least that Heaven may give.

And so, too, is the fifth stanza of the poem for the Sixth Sunday after Epiphany:

> So have I seen some tender flower
> Priz'd above all the vernal bower
> Shelter'd beneath the coolest shade,
> Embosom'd in the greenest glade,

> So frail a gem, it scarce may bear
> The playful touch of evening air;
> When hardier grown we live it less,
> And trust it from our sight, not needing our caress.

In this stanza by analogy to the flower of Nature, Keble traces our attitude towards the baby which grows up gradually and becomes accustomed to the world: again, he strikes a Wordsworthian note.

Besides Prince's 'imagery of the English countryside', Keble's poetry also shows evidence of much use made of imagery taken from the Bible; and in this sense more discussion is necessary later when it is observed that Keble's imagery leads him into the use of symbols. Meanwhile it is clear that, in agreement with Newman, *The Christian Year* was concerned with either natural or revealed religion which, after all, was what Bishop Butler's philosophical treatise was about.

2 *Comfort and Obscurity*

As already pointed out, Wordsworth certainly approved of *The Christian Year*, and Keble told Pusey that Wordsworth had once proposed to him that they should go over it together, 'with a view to correcting the English'; and Pusey quoted, in his Preface to Keble's *Occasional Papers and Reviews*, the lines Keble wrote in an old pocket-book, dated September 10 1823:

At Barrow Elm

> O that my spirit were a choir, a place
> Where holy thoughts might meet to sing Thy grace!
> So once it was, or seemed awhile, but now
> 'Tis dull and timeless all, I know not how;
> Faint cries, like little birds asleep in pain,
> Are now the most my music can attain.

G.W. Doane, similarly, saw the close relationship of Wordsworth's poetry to Keble's, and in his American edition of *The Christian Year* presented the following verses of Wordsworth for its dedication:

Yes, if the intensities of hope and fear
Attract us still, and passionate exercise
Of lofty thoughts, the way before us lies
Distinct with signs — through which, in fixed career,
As though a zodiac, moves the ritual year
Of England's Church — stupendous mysteries!
Which whose travels in her bosom, eyes
As he approaches them, with solemn cheer
Enough for us to cast a transient glance
The circle through.[8]

There can be no doubt that the most direct influence on Keble's poetry was Wordsworth: the poems themselves clearly show it, and the Lectures stressed the influence.

The idea of creating a collection of poems following the order of the Christian year came to Keble from the preachings of the Reverend John Miller:

It has been suggested with great probability that the exact title of the volume was borrowed from sermon IV, 'The Christian Year' of 'A Christian Guide for Plain People,' by the author's great friend, the Rev. J. Miller (Oxford, 1820). The sermon shows how the cycle of the Christian seasons tends to build up a practical religion in simple people.[9]

More authoritatively, however, Sir John Coleridge wrote:

I may as well state here, though out of place, the little fact, that the title of his great work was taken from the fourth Sermon in John Miller's 'Christian Guide'; he asked his permission for this, which was of course readily accorded. Certainly it was an excellent title for such a work.[10]

G.W. Doane, sermonising on the usefulness of the year's pattern as a basis for the arrangement of Keble's poems, wrote of, 'the arrangement of the "Christian" or ecclesiastical "Year" which forms its groundwork' as 'the string on which his pearls are hung'. This extract sets the tone for Doane's eulogy of Keble in his introduction to the American edition.[11]

He continued:

The author of these pieces, it has come incidentally to the knowledge of the Editor, while he holds the most honourable office of Professor of Poetry in the University of Oxford, is the exemplary and faithful pastor of a humble country congregation, and devotes himself unsparingly to the spiritual welfare of a rustic flock, in which there is scarcely a single family of rank or education.

It should be remembered that Keble was his father's curate at Fairford until his father's death in 1835, and it was not until later that year that Sir William Heathcote, for the second time, offered him the living of Hursley in the diocese of Winchester, which he then accepted.

Doane went on to comment: '... *The Christian Year* apart from its high poetical merit, is recommended most earnestly for its pure, affectionate, and elevating character, as a "family book".' He then quoted a passage to prove his point from *Scenes in our Parish,* by a Country Parson's Daughter.

'Then came the long quiet evening', writes one who can well estimate the various merits of a volume which she has done much to draw into general use, 'when some of us gathered, as closely as possible, round the bright fire, and listened, while one and another dear voice read some passage from Keble's *Christian Year*. Soothing, beautiful poetry! well calculated to lift the heart above the cares of this troublesome world, and to light the path with the sunshine of heaven.'

Certainly, *The Christian Year* was kept as a family book and read round the fireside: the statistics relating to its sales and Amy Cruse's evidence for its popularity (see *The Victorians and their Books,* London 1935) both help to substantiate the fact. Of course, the keen sense of locality, and the strong regard for home and its domestic surroundings, were important criteria in judging a poet's worth,[12] and consequently they were qualities embodied in his own poetry. The last stanza of the poem for the first Sunday in Lent would have appealed to the family circle of a typically nineteenth-century Christian household:

Sweet is the smile of home; the mutual look
　When hearts are of each other sure;
Sweet all the joys that crowd the household nook,
　The haunt of all affections pure;
Yet in the world e'en these abide, and me
　Above the world our calling boast:
Once gain the mountain-top, and thou art free:
Till then, who rest, presume; who turn to look, are lost.

The text for the dedication of this poem is: 'Haste thee, escape
thither; for I cannot do anything till thou be come thither.
Therefore the name of the city was called Zoar' (Genesis
XIX, 22). Keble was instructing his readers that, while the
happy hope is a place of comfort, and while the Church is the
proper place for the Christian on earth, they, nevertheless,
should not be satisfied with their lot, but must look beyond to
the place in God's presence which is far better. It is doubtful, at
least debatable, whether the ordinary family understood *The
Christian Year* in any real way that approached a total
perception or comprehension. It is more likely that the poems
created a sentimental glow of affection for the Church of God
and the qualities and virtues it stood for: from the poems, no
doubt, the average reader derived the feelings of encouragement, comfort or consolation. It is unlikely, for instance, that
the average reader appreciated the full implications of Keble
making the incident from Genesis applicable to the Christian of
his day in the nineteenth century. The Church likened to the
Old Testament city of Zoar, with the Angel of Wrath holding
his destructive hand until Mercy gave the sign, were intriguing
images to wonder at, but their total impact was likely to be
known only by those with considerable Biblical knowledge, and
by those who shared Keble's ideas about the purpose of the Old
Testament. In a letter to Sir John Coleridge, dated 22 June
1827, Keble explained his view of the Old Testament (it was
expanded in his manuscript *The Jewish Nation, and God's
Dealings with Them*):[13]

It seems clear to me, on reading over the Old Testament,
that the example of the Jews *as a nation*, is there held out
in such a way as to regulate and correct the religious

conduct of us Christians *as individuals*. The covenant with them collectively was a type of that made with us separately; and the faults into which they fell analogous to what may be expected, and to what we really experience, in our own private dealings with the Almighty; this, I suppose, is what makes the Old Testament, as a whole, so useful to be considered by every Christian.[14]

Nevertheless, many of the poems were easy to understand, and recommended themselves to the general reader because of the advice they offered, or the consolation they afforded for some of life's bitterness. A few of them **have** found their way into the repository of hymns which continue to be sung in churches today. Keble's 'Morning' and 'Evening' poems are representative of these poems. The 'Morning' poem has as its dedication: 'His compassions fail not. They are new every morning' (Lament, III, 22,23). The poem opens with stanzas in praise of Nature; an easy lyricism helps to describe God's world:

> Hues of the rich unfolding morn,
>
> - - -
>
> Thou restling breeze so fresh and gay,
> That dancest forth at opening day,
> And brushing by with joyous wing,
> Wakenest each little leaf to sing; —
>
> Ye fragrant clouds of dewy stream,
> By which deep grove and tangled stream
> Pay, for soft rains in season given,
> Their tribute to the genial heaven;

Keble gradually led his reader into the common scenes of life and taught them that they should see God in their everyday surroundings, and, at the same time, he sought to reconcile them to their particular position in life. He emphasised:

> New every morning is the love
> Our wakening and uprising prove;
> Through sleep and darkness safely brought,
> Restor'd to life, and power, and thought.

And he pointed out:

> If oun our daily course our mind
> Be set to hallow all we find,
> New treasures still, of countless price,
> God will provide for sacrifice.
>
> Old friends, old scenes, will lovelier be,
> As more of Heaven in each we see:
> Some softening gleam of love and prayer
> Shall dawn on every cross and care.

Keble did not describe a world in which familiarity bred contempt: rather the opposite. In a sense it was a Wordsworthian doctrine, put forward in the Preface to the *Lyrical Ballads*, which declared that the poet should light up familiar things. If Keble's reader were to search for God, he was sure to find Him, especially in familiar surroundings. Nor was it necessary to cut yourself off from the routine of ordinary life in order to commune with God: there was no need to seek out 'the cloister'd cell'. Rather:

> The trivial round, the common task,
> Would furnish all we ought to ask;
> Room to deny ourselves; a road
> To bring us, daily, nearer God.

And so, the poem ends with its last stanza representative of prayer:

> Only, O Lord, in Thy dear love,
> Fit us for perfect Rest above
> And help us, this and every day,
> To live more nearly as we pray.

There was no difficulty about understanding this poem; and in it was contained a supreme message of hope, and a quiet direction on holy living. The message of hope and encouragement, the confidence expressed that a person should find in his own humble surroundings the recognition and

presence of God, both helped to reconcile the reader's mind to
his particular lot. The sentiments of the poem lay partly in
Keble's background reading, of course, which added to his own
convictions, in books such as Jeremy Taylor's *Holy Living and
Dying*, in William Law's *Serious Call*, and in George Herbert's
poetry, all of which were in Keble's personal library, now
preserved at Keble College.

Similarly, the poem 'Evening', possessed the spirit of quiet
confidence and comfort in the face of possible fear and the
isolation of darkness:

> Sun of my soul! Thou Saviour dear,
> It is not night if Thou be near:
> Oh! may no earth-born cloud arise
> To hide Thee from Thy servant's eyes.

And likewise, the last stanza is a prayer:

> Come near and bless us when we wake,
> Ere through the world our way we take;
> Till in the ocean of Thy love
> We lose ourselves in Heaven above.

The poem 'Holy Baptism' shows Keble in a mood of reverent
and tender affection, something to which his admirers were
quick to refer, and often remarked. Its appeal was immediate to
the devotional spirit, and it was this poem which first attracted
G.W. Doane to *The Christian Year*. The last two stanzas stress
the value and importance of the little child in God's sight:

> O tender gem, and full of Heaven!
> Not in the twilight stars on high,
> Not in moist flowers at even
> See we our God so nigh.

> Sweet one, make haste and know Him too,
> Thine own adopting Father love,
> That like thy earliest dew
> Thy dying sweets may prove.

Again, Keble taught his reader that God is closer to the world in the newly baptised infant than in any other part of his creation. Such a poem would certainly have found its way into the motherly hearts of his female readers.

The certainty of man's redemption is made clear in the poem for the Twenty-second Sunday after Trinity; and, at the same time, it is emphasised that as Christ is pledged to save and forgive mankind, so man must forgive his brothers. The text at the beginning of the poem reads: 'Lord, how oft shall my brother sin against me, and I forgive him?' (St Matthew, XVIII, 21). Keble showed, as Wordsworth had done before him in the 'Immortality Ode', that the child grows into the world, and so farther and farther away from the presence of God.

> O blest restraint! more blessed range!
> Too soon the happy child
> His nook of homely thought will change
> For life's seducing wild.

And, although the following stanza did not appear in the manuscript nor in the first edition, Keble felt it necessary to make quite obvious the fact of man's waywardness and the necessity of **his** redemption by Christ.

> It must be so: else wherefore falls
> The Saviour's voice unheard,
> While from His pard'ning Cross he calls,
> 'O spare as I have spar'd?'

So the poem tells, once more in simple terms, the fact of man's sinfulness; 'Yes ransom'd sinner!' Keble reproached, but he was careful to show the forgiveness of Christ. Again, the poem consoled its reader.

In the poem for the Fourteenth Sunday after Trinity Keble was reproachful, too. His text was: 'And Jesus answering said, Were there not ten cleansed? but where are the nine? There are not found that returned to give glory to God, save this stranger' (St Luke, XVII, 17, 18). Keble certainly offered praise and consolation to the one who remained faithful and thankful to God, banishing somewhat the ingrate. The faithful could be sure of blessing:

> ...by Thy placid voice and brow,
> With healing first, with comfort now,
> Turn'd upon him, who hastes to bow
>   Before Thee, heart and knee;
> 'Oh! thou, who only wouldst be blest,
> 'On thee alone My blessing rest!
> 'Rise, go thy way in peace possess'd
>   'For evermore of Me.'

His readers would have appreciated this reassurance; but the poem as a whole is uncertain, and leads into areas of *The Christian Year* where syntax makes for a lack of clear expression, and therefore a lack of understanding. It is difficult to sort out exactly what the following images represent, for instance, in the second stanza:

> Then from afar on God we cry;
> But should the mist of woe roll by,
> Not showers across an April sky
>   Drift, when the storm is o'er

which leads into the third stanza,

> Faster than those false drops and few
> Fleet from the heart, a worthless dew.

Apart from instances of this sort where sense suffers because of inadequate expression, Keble's own mind was uncertain about the poem as a whole, as his various amendments show. In the manuscript two stanzas originally stood in place of the printed third, and the opening triplet of the fifth read:

> Not more astounding were the view
> Nor would it paint the heart more true
> Than did those solemn words and few ...

Yet, presumably the general tenor of the poem made itself felt in the reader's understanding. Not so simple as the 'Morning' or 'Evening' poems, the details remained obscure, partly because of bad syntax, and partly because of confusing images, but the drift of Keble's sentiments was appreciated. This was true of a number of Keble's poems.

Generally, difficulties of comprehension lie in syntactic inaccuracy or inadequacy rather than in complicated imagery. Provided that the reader of Keble's poems knew the Bible, and was observant of the natural world around him, imagery was not likely to raise any problems.

The best example of syntactic inadequacy, which was adversely criticised in Keble's own lifetime, is to be found in the poem for Septuagesima Sunday which is a good example too of Keble's reading of Butler. The second stanza is sufficient evidence of the latter point:

> The works of God above, below
> Within us and around,
> Are pages in that book, to show
> How God Himself is found.

So in the world around us we can learn to see God. However, the first stanza opens with the line, 'There is a book, who runs may read', which caused great concern in his own time. It is not self-evident, in its context, that the word 'runs' means more than it immediately seems to stand for. In fact, if the reader substitutes, in terms of sense, 'runs the course of life', or 'prospers in life', as the word is used in the book of Habbakuk, the proper meaning becomes quite clear. Nevertheless, it was a line which earned Keble some derision for inspiring an inappropriate image in the reader's mind.

Often, words which are ordinarily necessary for giving a sentence complete sense are left out, which similarly creates difficulty. One example occurs in 'Holy Baptism': the third stanza reads:

> A few calm words of faith and prayer,
> A few bright drops of holy dew,
> Shall work a wonder there
> Earth's charmers never knew.

The last two lines are meaningless until it is realised that 'where' is required before 'Earth's' to give complete sense. Another example of ellipsis causing obscurity is the first line of stanza six of the poem for the Nineteenth Sunday after Trinity, 'He knew not, but there are who know': with thought, it becomes apparent that for its sense, the line needs 'those' after 'are'. And again, sense difficulties are presented by the first three lines of the eight stanza of the poem for Sexagesima Sunday:

> If niggard Earth her treasure hide,
> To all but labouring hands denied,
> Lavish of thorns and worthless weeds alone,
> The doom is half in mercy given
> To train us in our way to heaven,
> And shew our lagging souls how glory must be won.

Clearly, the expression of the first three lines needs expansion in order to make the sense in any way plain.

However, those who cavil about syntax should take heed of Newman's stricture that too much attention to language for its own sake betrays not the true poet but merely the artist. In Keble's case, the true poet did make himself vulnerable to charges of obscurity because of his exercise of economy, or reserve, and because many people could not follow his detailed Biblical allusion: however, they did grasp, in a general way, the meaning of what he wrote. This was the source of their comfort.

3 *Reserve, Symbol, Metre and Diction*

Keble's prime purpose was to offer comfort in his poetry. He subtitled his Lectures 'De Poeticae Vi Medica': it was important that poetry should act as a balm for the troubled mind of the reader as well as of the poet himself. In the Advertisement at the beginning of *The Christian Year*, Keble wrote about 'that soothing tendency in the Prayer Book, which it is the chief purpose of these pages to exhibit'. Certainly every reader was not going to understand the significance of all the poems: they were not written in Wordsworth's 'selection of language really used by men'. The poems assumed a Biblical knowledge, especially of the Old Testament, and even of the Apocrypha, which most people did not have. Walter Lock in his edition *The Christian Year: with Introduction and Notes* published in 1898, conceded:

> The obscurity where it is to be found, is sometimes due to a mystical treatment of Holy Scripture, which is not so familiar to us as it used to be: more often it is due to the quick-darting thought of the writer, passing from one subject to another by a train of feeling rather than of logic.

The Times in its obituary notice of Keble proclaimed that: 'The Goliath of the Low Church party talked of Keble's "obscure lyrics", and asked what they were about.'

Total understanding of his poetry, apart from the occasional verses such as 'Fairford again' or 'To Master Bernard Wilson's Dog' collected in *Miscellaneous Poems*,[15] was, by Keble's own admission in his writing about the theory of poetry, impossible. Often his poetry plumbed some of the depths of mysticism, and in its turn became mystical, so earning for itself the strictures of many contemporary critics. Sydney Smith, the great Whig philanthropist, the founder of *The Edinburgh Review*, who ridiculed the Evangelicals, despised the Puseyites and was averse to all mysticism in literature or religion, said that 'portions of the book [*The Christian Year*] are puzzling'. A prominent bishop was reputedly supposed to have called Keble's poems his 'Sunday puzzle'. *The Times* obituary of Keble spoke of *The Christian Year* being 'too exclusively the manual of well-educated Church people'. It wondered what the average National School teacher would make of them, and gave the opinion that, 'of more than 100 poems only 20 are not absolutely obscure'. By a happy computation, it went on to say that there were '15 which could be mastered', and 'more than 70 are really only meant for people who, with a little aid, could make out the train of thought in a Greek Chorus'.

Nevertheless, William Temple in his memoir of Keble in his edition of *The Christian Year*[16] wrote that it was Keble's peculiar fortune and the result of *The Christian Year* that he was '... the first to rescue the Prayer Book and the Church services from the charges of formalism, under which they lay, to prove their powers of adaptation to modern wants, to bring to light the undercurrent of devotion and sympathetic helpfulness which pervades them'.

However true this was, Keble's poetry was very much in accord with what he laid down in his reviews and lectures. Poetry was a divine means through which God was made known to man, and the fact of his existence verified: it was the special means by which religious sense and knowledge could be imparted; and by its use the poet could come close to expressing any explanation of the mystery, which, he felt, necessarily lay at the back of Christianity. He did not worry that he might try to express, or penetrate, the mystery of Christianity at the expense of clarity. Mystical significance, the viability to explain the true nature of God, and an implicit faith which justified Christianity, were fundamental to Keble's religion. Owen Chadwick writes: 'Like poetry, the theological proposition was a door into a garden of Eden which could be glimpsed but not mapped.'[17] Rather it was the other way round. Keble preached the Doctrine of Reserve in the matter of the sublimities of religion: he took his example from the Early Fathers and as well as theorising about the doctrine as applied to poetry in his Lectures, he approved and recommended Isaac William's tract published in 1837 called *On Reserve in Communicating Religious Knowledge*.

In his Tract, Williams expressed one of the basic tenets of Tractarian Christianity: he explained the 'Disciplina Arcani', and reaffirmed the Doctrine of Reserve. He wrote about 'the strong indications which all must have noticed throughout St Paul's Epistles, and he discloses and witholds Christian Knowledge and mysteries, according to the meetness of those to whom he was writing to receive them'. He went on to say:

The Disciplina Arcani is spoken of, not as some ecclesiastical system founded on motives of expediency, as is now often supposed, or arising from the circumstances of the times, or as merely directed against heathens; it is implied that this reserve is an universal principle in morals; ... that it has the authority of our Lord Himself and His disciples; ... that an awful and reverential sense of His thus disclosing Himself only according to the state of man's heart is the only key to the knowledge of His ways, either in His moral providences or His more direct revelations.[18]

Later, Williams wrote of the good tradition, which the Tractarians had to follow in the Doctrine of Reserve, and which was to be found among the writings of the Early Church Fathers. He emphasised that St Chrysostom, 'speaks of it frequently as a rule important to be observed in communicating religious knowledge',[19] and he quoted St Cyril of Jerusalem:

> The sun renders blind the weak-sighted; not that it is the nature of the sun to make persons blind, but that the state of their eyes cannot bear its light. Thus it is that they whose hearts are diseased from unbelief, are not able to look upon the bright rays of Godhead. The Lord spake to those who were able to hear in parables, and those parables he explained privately to His disciples.[20]

Williams continued to describe the Hebrew language as one in which 'each word contains many deep and ulterior meanings, which may be considered as types of each other'. He reasoned:

> For if the sacred language which the Almighty has chosen in order to reveal Himself to mankind is of this typical nature, it proves that such is the language of God; that in numerous analogies and resemblances, differing in time, importance, and extent, but with one drift and scope, He is used to speak to us, blending figure with word spoken.[21]

At the end of the Tract, Williams firmly stated the Tractarian position:

> In the older dispensation He was ever as One who, in disclosing, hideth Himself. When our Lord appeared on earth in His incarnation, He was still ever as one who, ever desirous to manifest, yet in love for mankind withdrew Himself. The same was ever the case in His Church in its purest and best days; it was ever (as in faint imitation of her Lord) a system of reserve, in which the

blessings of the Kingdom were laid up, as a treasure hid in a field. And such is still the system of the Church throughout all her ways; God dwelleth in secret, and by faith only can be discerned. Faith is the key to His secret treasures.[22]

It is characteristic of Williams, and Keble too, that he should have rounded off the Tract with reference to contemporary affairs:

If we wish to do good to the world we must not look to it, but unto God; our strength must be in secret where God is; the bad instruments of the world (such as the daily periodical) must not be ours; the platform is not our strength, nay, even the pulpit itself is not our chief strength; in these we must yield to others if they wish it: but our chief strength must be the Altar; it must be in sacraments and prayers, and a good life to give efficacy to them.[23]

The popular press, and the oratory of the pulpit, were to be shunned: their methods of address were far too open and public.

In a very important way, William's Tract 87 stands as an embodiment of Keble's views. It was a summing up of Keble's position some ten years after the publication of *The Christian Year,* and it goes a long way to help explain Keble's mode of address to his poetic audience in the writing of his poems. It must be remembered that Keble gave his *imprimatur* to Williams's Tract. The arcane discipline was a very cornerstone to Keble's belief, and we must expect it to have had a very serious bearing on his poetry.

Subsequently, Keble made his own position clear in 1841 by publishing Tract 89, *On the Mysticism Attributed to the Early Fathers of the Church,* in which he defended the Church Fathers from wrong interpretations, and reverently explained the form of their Christianity: at the same time, he reinforced what Williams had already written, and, incidentally, explained the symbolism that lay behind his own poetry.

He showed again how many of the early saints believed in, and practised, the Doctrine of Reserve. He talked of St

Barnabas's writing, and, in many cases, of 'the sort of scruple, with which he imparts it, an instance of the discipline of reserve, which the Church recommended in the conveyance of all her mysteries'.[24] He quoted Origen's allegories as reconcilable with reserve, and stated:

> That it was by no means his custom, to trust his ordinary hearers with all the mysterious wonders, which he seemed to himself faintly to discern in Scripture, but that he always suggested those which he judged best for edifying: of which edification, one necessary groundwork would be, the securing the flock against the prevailing heresies.[25]

A little later, Keble wrote particularly about the nature of poetry, and saw mysticism as the equivalent of poetry for the Church:

> If we suppose Poetry in general to mean the expression of an overflowing mind, relieving itself, more or less indirectly and unreservedly, of the thoughts and passions which most oppress it: — on which hypothesis each person will have a Poetry of his own, a set of associations appropriate to himself for the works of nature and other visible objects, in themselves common to him with others — if this be so, what follows will not perhaps be thought altogether an unwarrantable conjecture; proposed, as it ought, and is wished to be, with all fear and religious reverence.[26]

In a similar war, Keble claimed, that, because of the incarnation, Christ would have his own Poetry.

> ... may it not be affirmed that he condescends in like manner to have a Poetry of His own, a set of holy and divine associations and meanings, wherewith it is His will to invest all material things? And the authentic records of His will, in this, as in all other truths are supernatural, are, of course, Holy Scripture, and the consent of ecclesiastical writers.[27]

Of course, the Doctrine of Reserve is most important for a proper understanding of Keble's poetry: he applied the doctrine to his poetry and so veiled what he had to impart from the gaze of the vulgar.

In his Lectures he praised Spenser as a true Christian poet who tried to instruct men to live as good Christians, to avoid the *accidie* of the Cave of Despair, and the idle pleasures of the Bower of Bliss. For his purpose, Spenser had used allegory and symbol. The vulgar could not fully appreciate the truth: instruction and mediation were needed in order that the veil should be lifted and the mystery penetrated. An echo of Spenser is shown in the poem 'Forward':[28]

> The Christian knows his time is short,
>   But oh! the way is rough and drear;
> And bowers of bliss are nigh, to court
>   His spirits from its high career.

This poem 'composed during a hard trot on the Witney road, on a Monday morning, March, 1818' was straightforward enough, but elsewhere the veil shields the uninitiated from the sacred truth. In the poem for Trinity Sunday the principle of hidden truth is elaborated. There is a direct parallel to man's fate living on earth: he is unable to see God: he is allowed only to catch glimpses of Him during his earthly existence. So the poem's dedication is the text: 'If I have told you earthly things, and ye believe not, how shall ye believe, if I tell you of heavenly things?, (St John, III, 12). Keble called upon God, 'Creator, Saviour, strengthening Guide' that He might:

> Help us, each hour, with steadier eye
> To search the deepening mystery
> The wonders of thy sea and sky.

The journey through life to God's presence, Keble expressed thus:

> As travellers on some woodland height,
> When wintry suns are gleaming bright,
> Lose in arch'd glades their tangled sight; —

> By glimpses such as dreamers love
> Through her grey veil the leafless grove
> Shews where the distant shadows rove; —

> Such trembling joy the soul o'er-awes
> As nearer to Thy shrine she draws: —
> And now before the choir we pause.

Man's progress to God's presence, to the 'shrine', is gradual and only glimpses are given through the grove's veil, of shadows that move beyond close to the desired goal; but it would be unbearable for the soul to approach suddenly the awful presence. The image of the woodland scene is fused with the symbol of the church building, approaching the altar along the various stages of the aisle until the choir is reached.

The clearest example of the Doctrine of Reserve at work in Keble's poetry is to be found in the poem for the Fourth Sunday in Lent. Here, the rose stands as a symbol for the way in which Christianity reveals itself in the world. Again the idea of the veil is used; and here Keble applied it to Nature:

> When Nature tries her finest touch
>   Weaving her vernal wreath,
> Mark ye, how close she veils her round,
> Not to be trac'd by sight or sound,
>   Nor soil'd by ruder breath?

There, in the last line, is an expression of Keble's constant anxiety over the vulgarisation of holy and respected things. Keble went on to ask:

> Who ever saw the earliest rose
>   First open her sweet breast?

He pointed out that:

> The gazing eye no change can trace,
> But look away a little space,
>   Then turn, and, lo! 'tis there.

Then he drew his analogy:

> But there's sweeter flower than e'er
>   Blush'd on the rosy spray —
> A brighter star, a richer bloom
> Than e'er did western heaven illume
>   At close of summer day.

This was Love, 'the last best gift of Heaven'; it was, 'gentle, holy, pure'.

But it is the last stanza which is the most explicit about the symbolism. The rose represents the true religion of Christ, and the device reflects clearly Keble's use of reserve in poetry:

> No — let the dainty rose awhile
>   Her bashful fragrance hide —
> Rend not her silken veil too soon,
> But leave her, in her own soft noon,
>   To flourish and abide.

Obviously, there was much in what *The Times* obituary had to say about 'well-educated Church people' alone being able to grasp the meaning of Keble's poetry. Another example is found in the poem for the Fifteenth Sunday after Trinity. The lily is the subject of poetic meditation and becomes the symbol for divine knowledge and a calm earthly serenity:

> The stars of heaven a course are taught
> Too high above our human thought;
> Ye may be found if ye are sought,
>   And as we gaze, we know.

Later, Keble stressed that although a quest is needed to seek out the qualities which the lily displays, it must not be made in a spirit of pride: rather humility is necessary:

> Nor may we scorn, too proudly wise,
> Your silent lessons, undescried
>   By all but lowly eyes.

Finally, Keble showed in the last stanza how few people succeeded; and this was a cause for grief, and something which perhaps his poem could remedy:

> Alas! of thousand bosoms kind,
> That daily court you and caress,
> How few the happy secret find
> Of your calm loveliness!

It is Tract 89 which helps the reader to see beyond the veil of reserve and which is most helpful for the interpretation of Keble's symbolism. In it he relies firmly on examples from the Bible and examples used by the Early Church Fathers. So the whole of the visible world exists as a type of the invisible: again, there is an echo of Butler's philosophy. For Keble, in the Bible was a ready, formulated system of imagery, which extended further to provide a pattern of symbols. In Tract 89, Keble carefully analysed the mystical significance of the visible world. The sky represents 'a canopy spread over the tents and dwellings of the saints', birds are tokens of 'Powers in heaven above who watch our proceedings in this lower world', and waters flowing into the sea are 'people gathered into the Church of Christ'.[29] The smell of flowers represents 'the odour of sanctity', tares and weeds, 'false principles', the tamarisk, 'the double mind', the palm, 'eternal purity', and the Heavenly bodies are a well-known set of symbols.

> The Sun, the greater light, is our Lord; the Noon, the lesser light, the Church. '"He appointed the moon for certain seasons, and the Sun knoweth his going down." This place,' St Ambrose tells us, 'appears to be commonly understood in a mystical sense concerning Christ and his Church.'[30]

The stars are representative of the saints in Heaven. Keble continued with his parallels: silkworm/token of the Resurrection, turtle-dove/chaste and holy widowhood, the wolf/the Evil One.[31]

With Keble's explanation of his scheme of symbols in Tract 89, it is much easier to understand the proper significance of his poetry. Clearly, the Bible offered him his scheme of symbolism, and working from Tract 89, bearing in mind always the epigraph to each poem, it is possible to interpret the symbols, penetrate the veil, and work through the reserve. At the same time, it must be remembered that Keble's poetry relied not only on religious symbolism embodied in the Bible, but also on natural symbolism embodied in English poetry: by these means, the moral core of Keble's poetry was sustained.

The poem for Septuagesima Sunday explicitly supports Keble's analysis in Tract 89:

> The Moon above, the Church below,
>   A wondrous race they run,
> But all their radiance, all their glow,
>   Each borrows of its Sun.
>
> The Saviour lends the light and heat
>   That crowns His holy hill;
> The saints, like stars, around His seat,
>   Perform their courses still.
>
> The saints above are stars in Heaven —
>   What are the saints on earth?
> Like trees they stand whom God has given,
>   Our Eden's happy birth.

It is necessary to remember that this poem was written in 1819, and it is significant in showing Keble's constant regard to the writings of the Early Church Fathers that much of the phrasing used to explain symbols in the Tract is the same as that used in this early poem.

The poem for the Third Sunday after Trinity, prefaced by the text 'There is joy in the presence of the angels of God over one sinner that repenteth' (St Luke, XV 10), is a good example of Keble's use of Biblical and natural imagery which has, at the same time, symbolical significance. Keble writes of the first flowers of the wood which are unseen by man, and expresses the Doctrine of Reserve in stanzas five and six:

He in the mazes of the budding wood
    Is near, and mourns to see our thankless glance
Dwell coldly, where the fresh green earth is strew'd
    With the first flowers that lead the vernal dance.

In wasteful bounty shower'd, they smile unseen,
    Unseen by man — but what if purer sprights
By moonlight o'er their dewy bosoms lean
    To adore the Father of all gentle lights?

Here, there is an identification of God with Nature: he dwells with the first flowers of the wood; and, in turn, the flowers, symbols of Heavenly sanctity, cannot be seen by ordinary men, but, no doubt, there are saintlier spirits who can perceive them.

B.M. Lott has listed a number of specifically Biblical symbols:[32] he notes 'flame' meaning the Holy Spirit in the poem for Thursday before Easter, 'cup' meaning suffering in the poem for St James's day. Elsewhere equivalents exist: spring/resurrection (Holy Baptism), dove/Holy Ghost (confirmation), sword/admonition Second Sunday after Easter), and dew/mercy (Holy Baptism). He detects, too, images which are not particularly Biblical, but, in a limited sense, more original: he cites, anchor/cross, music/job, gospel tears/Jesus's blood, dog days/middle age, and fallen sister/the Roman Catholic Church.

Lott makes an important point that the Industrial Revolution had made it extremely plain that country life should be praised and followed. Keble recognised this fact, and wrote the poem for St Matthew: it shows much of the conventional clash between 'urbs' and 'rus'. However, yet again, Keble can fall back on available Biblical symbolism: Babel represents the city, and paradise, country life. The last two stanzas are:

These gracious lines shed Gospel light
    On Mammon's gloomiest cells,
As on some city's cheerless night
    The tide of sun-rise swells,
Till tower, and dome, and bridge-way proud
Are mantled with a golden cloud,
And to wise hearts this certain hope is given;
'No mist that man may raise, shall hide the eye of Heaven.'

And oh! if e'en on Babel shine
     Such gleams of Paradise,
Should not their peace be peace divine,
     Who day by day arise
To look on clearer heavens, and scan
The work of God untouch'd by man?
Shame on us, who about us Babel bear,
And live in Paradise, as if God was not there!

Clearly, with an understanding of the Biblical significance of Keble's imagery in this example, the didactic point of his poem is obvious; and combined with a consideration of the poem's epigraph, as with so many of Keble's poems, there remains no difficulty in understanding what Keble meant.

One symbol which Keble used, and which was remarked by Prince in his *Leading Ideas of Keble's* 'Christian Year', (see p.123) is that of falling, dying leaves. Prince thinks that they are symbols of resignation; but rather they are symbols of decaying life unblessed by anything similar to man's redemption. In the poem for the Twenty-third Sunday after Trinity, Keble wrote:

Yet wait awhile, and see the calm leaves float
     Each to his rest beneath their present shade.

How like decaying life they seem to glide!
     And yet no second spring have they in store,
But where they fall, forgotten to abide
     Is all their portion, and they ask no more.

In another poem, that for the First Sunday after Easter, the image is used again, in a stanza which emphasises fusion of natural and religious imagery in Keble's verse:

O joys, that sweetest in decay
Fall not, like wither'd leaves, away,
     But with the silent breath
Of violets drooping one by one,
Soon as their fragrant task is done,
     Are wafted high in death!

Although the image of falling leaves in autumn is commonplace enough, it is interesting to note that the Oxford theologian and classicist, Gerard Manley Hopkins, used it as a symbol for dying people in his poem 'Spring and Fall':

> Margaret are you grieving
> Over Goldengrove unleaving?
> Leaves, like the things of man, you
> With your fresh thoughts care for, can you?

Perhaps there is a tenuous connection here which might indicate some influence, on the part of Keble's writing, on Hopkins and his own very religious theory of poetry: it should be remembered that the windhover represented Christ, and pied beauty reflected the glory of God.

The last words in the matter of symbolism should be Keble's own. At the end of Tract 89, he declared:

> Poetry traced as high up as we can go, may almost seem to be God's gift from the beginning, vouchsafed to us for this very purpose: at any rate the fact is unquestionable, that it was the ordained vehicle of Revelation, until God Himself was made manifest in the flesh. And since the characteristic tendency of poetical minds is to make the world of sense, from the beginning to end, symbolical of the absent and unseen, any instance of divine favour shewn to Poetry, any divine use of it in the training of God's people, would seem, as far as it goes, to warrant that tendency; to set God's seal upon it, and witness it as reasonable and true.[33]

In connection with Keble's conscious acknowledgement of the Doctrine of Reserve in poetic composition, his opinions on the use of metre and rhyme should be noted. Clearly, he abided by the use of classical forms of metre; and it was closely associated with his idea of the nature of poetry. Part of the purpose of poetry was to express the poet's inmost feelings which he could no longer contain unless he was to risk madness. Poetry was the form of expression in which he might speak out, and at the same time not expose himself to the vulgar gaze. In the review of Lockhart's *Life of Sir Walter Scott*[34] Keble wrote:

> ...the very task of metrical arrangement will fall in with
> the poetical instinct, such as has been above described, in
> two respects. On the one hand, it shapes out a sort of
> channel for wild and tumultuous feelings to vent them-
> selves by; feelings whose very excess and violence would
> seem to make the utterance of them almost impossible, for
> the very throng of thoughts and words, crowding all at
> once to demand expression. In such cases, the
> conventional rules of metre and rhythm may evidently
> have the effect of determining, in some one direction, the
> overflow of sentiment and expression, wherewith the mind
> might otherwise be fairly oppressed. On the other hand,
> the like rules may be no less useful, in throwing a kind of
> veil over those strong or deep emotions, which need relief
> but cannot endure publicity. The very circumstance of
> their being expressed in verse draws off attention from the
> violence of the feelings themselves, and enables people to
> say things which they could not venture in prose, much
> in the same way as the musical accompaniment gives
> meaning to the gestures of the dance, and hinders them
> from appearing to the bystanders merely fantastic. This
> effect of metre seems quite obvious as far as regards the
> sympathies of others.

Pusey referred the readers of the *Occasional Papers* to the
stanza from 'Stammering' in *Lyra Innocentium:*

> When heart and head are both o'erflowing,
> When eager words within are glowing,
> And all at once for utterance crowd and throng,
> How hard to find no tongue.

So the idea of reserve applied to poetry was twofold: it shielded
precious truths from the uninitiated and vulgar; and it shielded
the poet from the glare of unwelcome publicity.

Keble's choice of diction, too, managed to keep poetry apart
from the ordinary and the mundane. It was not necessary to
write in everyday language: it was fitting that poetry should

have its own specialised, esoteric vocabulary. In this way, the veil was even more firmly secured. Therefore, in the matter of diction Keble did not agree with Wordsworth, but looked backwards to the eighteenth century, and farther, especially to the language of Milton's minor poems. Almost everywhere in Keble's poetry the quality of diction is artificial and archaic: it is certainly not the sort of language which Wordsworth wanted to be used in describing nature; it is much more in keeping with the poetic vocabulary of especially the eighteenth-century poets prior to Blake, which Wordsworth said, in his Preface to *The Lyrical Ballads*, he wanted to reject. Keble may have rescued church services from the charges of formalism, as William Temple claimed, but he did not do anything about rescuing poetic diction from the formalism which Wordsworth described.

A typical example of Keble's use of diction appears in the first three stanzas of the poem for Tuesday in Easter Week, subtitled 'To the Snowdrop'. Walter Lock recorded that the poem was not written down in the manuscript notebooks, but a copy is found in a letter of Keble to his sister dated 10 March 1826:

> Thou first-born of the year's delight,
>   Pride of the dewy glade,
> In vernal green and virgin white,
>   Thy vestal robes, array'd:
>
> 'Tis not because thy drooping form
>   Sinks graceful on its nest,
> When chilly shades from gathering storm
>   Affright thy tender breast:
>
> Nor for yon river islet wild
>   Beneath the willow spray,
> Where, like the ringlets of a child,
>   Thou weav'st thy circle gay.

In this extract the ring of convention is plainly heard echoing through words such as 'thou', 'vernal', 'vestal', ''tis', 'affright', 'yon', and 'weav'st'.

Elsewhere Keble's archaisms stand out. He used the word

'fain' excessively:

> We too, O lord, would fain command
> (First Sunday after Christmas)

> And thou, too curious ear, that fain
> Wouldst thread the maze of Harmony
> (Fourth Sunday in Advent)

> The wilful heart be fain to own
> That he ...
> (Second Sunday after Christmas)

> Is fain to slake its fire.
> (Second Sunday after Epiphany)

> Thy Church is fain to cry.
> (Fifth Sunday after Epiphany)

> Deafens the ear that fain would wake.
> (Fourth Sunday after Trinity)

> Was fain to look to Heaven and sigh.
> (Twelfth Sunday after Trinity)

and these are only some of the references in *The Christian Year* alone. In the poem for Easter Day, Keble used the archaic word 'fane' for temple: 'Tis now a fane, where Love can find'.

Another archaism, belonging entirely to the stock of poetic vocabulary was the word 'vernal'. It appears in the last two lines of the poem for the 'Circumcision of Christ':

> And seems it hard, thy vernal years
> Few vernal joys can show?

and Keble used it repeatedly:

> But vernal airs ...
> (Third Sunday after Easter)

> The primrose in her vernal nest.
> (Seventh Sunday after Trinity)

although he did change the word from a manuscript reading of 'vernal shower' in the poem for the Fourth Sunday after Easter to:

But ne'er so soft fell noon-tide shower.

Elsewhere Keble used copiously words such as 'Lo', ''Twas', 'e'en', as well as those already mentioned: but perhaps the most obtrusive archaism is found in the poem for the Seventh Sunday after Trinity where Keble made use of the word 'cates': 'No cates ambrosial are supplied'. Like many of the archaisms, this word can be traced back to Elizabethan usage which, in part, was revived by Keats; and since it is inconceivable that such a well-read man as Keble could be unaware of Keat's poetry, it is almost certain that Keble was in some measure, influenced by Keats. The poem in which 'cates' appears was written on 4 November 1825.

With these conscious archaisms, and his continual personifications of abstractions, for instance 'Ambition' and 'Folly' in the poem for the Monday in Whitsun-Week, Keble was being conventional in style and diction, looking backwards through Gray to Milton, and setting his poetry apart from vulgar usage: the 'Elegy written in a Country Churchyard' reads: 'Let not Ambition mock their useful toil.' The direct copy of the form of Gray's great Elegy in the poem for the Twenty-third Sunday after Trinity, has already been mentioned (see p. 70). In the poem for the Third Sunday in Lent is more evidence of Keble's regard for Gray: there occurs the line: 'Fly from the "old poetic fields",' which is undoubtedly a reference to Gray's: 'Where each old poetic mountain Inspiration breath'd around', from 'The Progress of Poesy'. In manuscript Keble's poem was called 'The Spoils of Satan', but the title was omitted on publication. The fourth stanza is an example of Keble's extravagance which went out of control, so creating a baroque image: he wrote of 'bowers of balm', 'billowy corn', 'tresses of the plain', and rounded off the stanza with the Gothic image of 'some towers of giants old'. Later, in the same poem, he wrote: 'It was a fearful joy, I ween,' and: 'Ye Paynim shadows dark.'

It was as though the use of antiquated language were to invest his poems with more authority and worth than they would otherwise have possessed.

It is curious that Keble's ear rejected the use of the old word 'wilder': on at least three occasions he replaced it. In the editions, he sanctioned: 'Thy course in Earth's bewildering ways' (Thursday before Easter), while in the manuscript he had written: 'More closely thine own wildered ways.' He printed 'Or lawless roam around this earthly waste' (Ascension Day) for the manuscript version: 'Or wildering roam ...'. And he passed 'Pray only that thine aching heart' (Eleventh Sunday after Trinity), in place of the manuscript reading: 'Pray only that thy wildered heart.'

Yet this sort of vocabulary combined with Biblical diction and imagery, arising from Keble's close Scriptural scholarship and from Milton's poetry, combined to set the poetry at a distance from the minds of ordinary people in the matter of total understanding: this is not to say that his poetry was unimpressive, or failed to catch the imagination, or failed to proclaim the message of spiritual comfort. So it was with the poem for Whitsunday:

> Like arrows went those lightnings forth
> > Wing'd with the sinner's doom,
> But these, like tongues, o'er all the earth
> > Proclaiming life to come:
>
> And as on Israel's awe-struck ear
> > The voice exceeding loud,
> The trump, that angels quake to hear,
> > Thrill'd from the deep, dark cloud;
>
> So, when the Spirit of our God
> > Came down His flock to find,
> A voice from Heaven was heard abroad,
> > A rushing mighty wind.

Clearly, poetry that was the handmaid of religion was going to be seriously influenced by the Bible; and since the poet was priest, too, his verses were bound to have a ministering effect on his readers.

4 *Relationship with Other Poets, and 'de Poeticae vi Medica'.*
Other influences on Keble's poetry are easily discernible, and
many reflect his opinions expressed in the Lectures. A
publication called *The New Christian Year: with the Old Poets*
(London, 1855), edited by H.E.M.[35] gave selections of poetry
from Keble's forerunners, and among them can be traced a
number of sources and models for some of his poems. There are
marks and traces of Keble's poetic masters and betters
throughout his poetry, some of which have already been
mentioned: for example, Spenser and Milton. Spenser was
certainly one of Keble's favourite poets, and he is undoubtedly
glimpsed having an influence on the imagery of the poem for
Tuesday in Whitsun Week. The 'Fairie Queene's' red-cross
knight must have been prominent in Keble's mind when he
wrote:

> And wheresoe'er in earth's wide field,
> Ye lift, for Him, the red-cross shield,
> Be this your song, your joy and pride —
> 'Our Champion went before and died.'

However, the influence of Milton's minor poems, despite what
Keble thought of Milton as a man, represented a more
dominant influence. In the poem for the Second Sunday in
Advent, which starts off well enough with a stanza typical in
many ways of Keble's poetry, showing his reliance on the
images of nature, his easy rhymes, his tender sentiment, his
archaic diction and elisions (o'er, ere, flow'rets, th'uncertain),
the mark of Milton is at once plain:

> Not till the freezing blast is still
> Till freely leaps the sparkling rill,
> And gales sweep soft from summer's skies,
> As o'er a sleeping infant's eyes
> A mother's kiss; ere calls like these,
> No sunny gleam awakes the trees,
> Nor dare the tender flow'rets show
> Their bosoms to th'uncertain glow.

There is a suspicion of exaggerated tenderness, and a hint of inappropriateness in the simile likening the summer's gales to a mother's kisses of her infant's sleeping eyes. A little later in the poem Keble misquoted Milton, perhaps in order to accommodate his rhyme: he wrote:

> Christ watches by a Christian's hearth,
> Be silent, 'vain deluding mirth',
> Till in thine alter'd voice be known
> Somewhat of Resignation's tone.

'Il Penseroso' has 'vain deluding joys', and Keble not only changes a word in Milton's phrase, but he plagiarises one of Milton's rhymes:

> Far from all resort of mirth,
> Save the Cricket on the hearth.

The Miltonic ring is again heard in the lines of the poem for the First Sunday in Lent, not only in the Old Testament imagery of the 'Angel of Wrath', the book of Genesis and the city of Zoar, but also in the rhythmical movement of the poem's metre. Lines such as,

> Lingering in heart, and with frail sidelong eye,
> Seeking how near they may unharm'd remain,

are reminiscent of the metrical beat achieved in some lines of 'Paradise Lost', and so is the syntactical inversion of the second line.

In the poem 'Morning', it is interesting to note the almost certain source of influence as Marvell's poem 'To his Coy Mistress', even though the rhyme 'run/sun', like 'moon/June', is one of the most recurrent in English poetry. The four lines appear in manuscript and were printed in the first proof, but were finally omitted from the first edition:

> Hence the poor sinner still has found
> Life but one dull unvarying round,
> And mourned ere half his course was run
> That 'nought is new beneath the sun'.

The sentiment was proverbial, and often occurs in the work of another of Keble's favourite poets, Chaucer: he frequently stated that there is no such thing as 'newfanglednesse'. But the metre and rhyme of Keble's lines were the same as the last couplet of Marvell's poem:

> Thus, though we cannot make our sun
> Stand still, yet we will make him run.

Keble's debt to George Herbert has already been alluded to, and has been studied in a comparison between *The Christian Year* and *The Temple* written by E.N.S. Thompson.[36]

Keble found in Herbert's poetry sound Christian thinking, agreeable   sentiments, themes which appealed to Keble's like mind and a recourse to Biblical imagery which Keble approved; and constantly Herbert's poems make analogy to the Church and its fabric. Such a poem as Herbert's 'Church-rents and schisms' in which the rose is symbol for the Universal Church must have pleased Keble. At the end of the first stanza, the rise is spoiled:

> ...Onely shreds of thee,
> And those all bitten, in thy chair I see.

Such was the condition of the church as Herbert saw it. For the rest of the poem Herbert refers to the church as 'Mother', as Keble does often in his poetry, for example in the one for the Seventeenth Sunday after Trinity:

> ...O Mother dear
> Wilt thou forgive thy son one boding sigh?

Elsewhere too, Herbert had given Keble models for symbolism. 'The Flower' showed Spring as a symbol for resurrection, and 'The Sonne', in a fine piece of metaphysical playing with words:

> How neatly doe we give one onely name
> To parents issues and the sunnes bright starre!

relates the 'Sonne of Man' with the sun. In such examples, the

parallel in ideas and imagery between Keble's poetry and
Herbert's is obvious, although Keble's poems lack the energy
and dexterity of Herbert's.

In other places, Keble's poetry followed Herbert's example in
exploring the fabric and building of a church. In the poem for
Trinity Sunday, the soul, approaching the presence of God, is
likened to a person approaching the altar in a church:

> The door is clos'd — but soft and deep
> Around the awful arches sweep
> Such airs as soothe a hermit's sleep.
>
> From each carv'd nook and fretted bend
> Cornice and gallery seem to send
> Tones that with seraph hymns might blend.
>
> Three solemn parts together twine
> In harmony's mysterious line;
> Three solemn aisles approach the shrine.

Herbert's imagery and symbolism, and the tone of his poetry,
appealed directly to Keble; and the Anglicanism which
prevades his poetry coincided with Keble's beliefs. It was
impossible for Herbert to fail as a serious influence on Keble. In
the *Lectures on Poetry*, Keble declared in admiration that
Herbert hid 'the deep love of God which consumed him behind a
cloud of precious conceits'.[37]

The Lectures acknowledge Keble's debt to other poets of past
centuries; but the major influences lay with the poets of his own
century and the end of the eighteenth century. Certainly there
are traces of Robert Burns: for instance, in the poem for the
Third Sunday in Lent:

> There's not a strain to Memory dear,
>   Nor flower in classic grove,
> There's not a sweet note warbled here,
>   But minds us of Thy Love.

The lines are very reminiscent of the lilt of Burn's 'Of A' the
Airts' written for his wife.

Whether or not Keble would have read Blake's poetry, at least before 1827, is debatable, but there are occasions when Blake's themes might have held significance for Keble. The poem for the Second Sunday after Epiphany showed Keble writing about childish innocence which becomes blighted by experience; but the thought might easily have been inspired by Wordsworth:

> The heart of childhood is all mirth
> We frolic to and fro
> As free and blithe, as if on earth
> Were no such thing as woe.

The answer to experience, in Keble's terms, both for Keble and his readers, is the consolation of the love of God and of the Redemption, the fact that Christ saved mankind from death, through death.

Keats, too, apart from the choice of archaic diction previously mentioned, seems to have exerted some influence. For instance, Keble often wrote of 'Fancy':

> ...light Fancy's reed,
> (Third Sunday in Advent)

more bitterly in the poem for Good Friday:

> But we by Fancy may assuage
> The festering sore by Fancy made,

and:

> To Fancy's eye their motions prove
> They mantle round the Sun for love.
> Second Sunday after Trinity)

It is possible from Keble's tone that he had in mind Keat's poem on Fancy, and therefore his conception of Fancy. In other places, there are lines which recall Keats. The 'wintry heaven and chill night air', and the 'music', 'light' and 'prayer' in the ninth stanza of the poem for Christmas Day, recall the stanzas which set the atmosphere for 'The Eve of St. Agnes'; and 'By these her thrilling minstrelsies' (Tuesday in Whitsun Week) recalls parts of 'Endymion'. The 'bleak hill-side' of Keble's poem for the Third Sunday after Epiphany, and the 'cold hill-side' of Keat's 'La Belle Dame sans Merci', are sufficiently similar in tone to lend evidence to the theory that Keat's sense of the medieval, as well as Scott's, was important to, and of some influence on, Keble, even though his personal library does not hold a copy of Keats's works.

Yet by far the most powerful influence on Keble's poetry, which can readily be appreciated from a reading of the Lectures, was without doubt, Wordsworth. The motto chosen for *Lyra Innocentium* was the last stanza of 'Anecdote for Fathers':

> O dearest, dearest boy! my heart
> For better love would seldom yearn,
> Could I but teach the hundredth part
> Of what from thee I learn.

The very idea of a *Lyra Innocentium* was of course, Wordsworthian (see p.81) songs not meant for children to sing or recite, but essentially about children written particularly for parents. It was hoped that this volume published in 1846, would do as well as *The Christian Year*, and so raise funds for the rebuilding of Hursley Church. On 20 August 1846, Keble wrote to his brother: 'Have we told you that I have heard from Parker about a 2nd Edition of L.I. It is to be of 3000 at 3/6d and I am to have £150 down — unless he refuses my terms. This is good news for Hursley Church.'[38] After the more strident tone of the *Lyra Apostolica*, the poems of *Lyra Innocentium* returned to the same style and moods of *The Christian Year*. The latter's poems have much of Wordsworth's philosophy about them. In the poem for the Second Sunday in Advent Keble described the Church as possessing a 'meditative eye' with which she looks on the objects of Nature; and all the poems reflect in some way, the power which Keble believed Nature to have that brought alive to people the real presence of God on earth:

> Where the landscape in its glory
> Teaches truth to wandering men.
> (First Sunday after Epiphany)

The Epiphany poems and the Easter poems especially are notable as Nature poems bearing the obvious Wordsworthian influence:

> Go up and watch the new-born rill
> Just trickling from its mossy bed,
>   Streaking the heath-clad hill
>   With bright emerald thread
>   (Monday in Easter Week)

or:

> See the soft green willow springing
>   Where the waters gently pass,
> Every way her free arms flinging
>   O'er the moist and reedy grass,
> Long ere winter blasts are fled,
> See her tipp'd with vernal red
> And her kindly flower display'd
> Ere her leaf can cast a shade.
>   (First Sunday after Epiphany)

However, although Wordsworth's influence was a pervading one, and spreads throughout Keble's poetry, not all the Romantic poets made a similar impression. Burns, while he had fine qualities, was censured in Keble's *Lectures on Poetry* as a man 'embittered with his misfortunes', someone who exhibited 'a mad and truly reckless craving for pleasure'. Byron, who 'sullied his splendid powers by many serious vices, inexcusable in anyone, to say nothing of a great poet', was a vain man, in Keble's view, and so was Shelley (see pp.99-101). As remarked, Keble found it difficult to forgive Scott for being on any sort of terms with Byron. Keble was pleased, nevertheless, to write down what Sir Walter Scott once told a Captain Hall. Hall reported:

Lord Byron quoted, with the bitterest despair, to Scott, the strong expression of Shakespeare, 'Our pleasant vices are but whips to scourge us'; he added, 'I would to God I could have your peace of mind, Mr Scott;

I would give all I have, all my fame, everything, to be able to speak on this subject' (that of domestic happiness) 'as you do.'

Keble believed that poetry was the means of preserving people 'from mental disease': it was a kind of safety valve. He agreed with Aristotle that the poet is possessed by some overpowering emotion which requires the relief of expression in order to prevent it terminating in madness. Keble's *Lectures on Poetry* were designated 'de poeticae vi medica'; and, as already pointed out, Keble wished his poems to support the soothing tendency of the Prayer Book. Yet what was critical to Keble's theory of poetry was that the poet had to compose or go mad, frenzied by the pent-up emotions inside him. It was essentially a private experience: a poet's expression was supposed to serve his own private purpose: the calming effect was foremost for the poet himself. As shown previously, Keble was reluctant to make public his poems: he was rather persuaded to it; and, no doubt, many of his poems represent highly tensed emotions which have been allowed private expression, restrained by rhyme and metre. In Keble's case, according to his arguments, a severe religious neurosis was avoided by his feelings overflowing into verse. So, the poem for Good Friday allows Keble an emotional catharsis when he was mentally preoccupied with Christ's crucifixion. The powerful cry of the last two stanzas are sufficient proof of this:

> Lord of my heart, by Thy last cry,
>   Let not Thy blood on earth be spent —
> Lo, at Thy feet I fainting lie,
>   Mine eyes upon Thy wounds are bent,
> Upon Thy streaming wounds my weary eyes
> Wait like the parched earth on April skies.
>
> Wash me, and dry these bitter tears,
>   O let my heart no further roam
> 'Tis Thine by vows, and hopes, and fears,
>   Long since — O call Thy wanderer home;
> To that dear home, safe in Thy wounded side,
> Where only broken hearts their sin and shame may hide.

On the other hand, there is the occasional poem, such as the one for Monday in Easter Week, composed on 12 February 1826 in order to complete the calendar arrangement of *The Christian Year*, written in a much more objective way.

For the most part, his poems were the effusions of an overburdened mind, certainly self-expressive, not as Alba Warren denies,[39] and protected from vulgar eyes by modesty, reserve, symbol, esoteric diction, metre and anonymity.

It is necessary to bear in mind that at first Keble was a reluctant publisher, although he became less reticent after the success of *The Christian Year*. In this principle, he differed from his mentor, Wordsworth, whose expressive theory of poetry M.H. Abrams describes in *The Mirror and the Lamp*.[40] For Wordsworth, it was essential that his poetry was public: it was necessary, in his view, that he should communicate his feelings to others. This was of secondary importance to Keble. The primary 'soothing tendency' was on the poet's own mind in a completely private way: any sympathetic process towards others was incidental.

In the *Lectures on Poetry*, Keble eventually reached the point, in Chapter XXIV, where he expressed distrust of the lyric poet because he considered him subject to moods and insincere passions, and came to regard dramatic and epic poets as essentially of Primary rank. Keble stated that the poet's intimate feelings:

> ... take refuge as it were in a kind of sanctuary, behind a veil, and shrink from the full light of day. Now, in the case of those who set themselves to weave a regular plot, I mean dramatic and epic poets, it is obvious that the composer's personality naturally holds itself apart and retires into the background. Opinions are expressed, judgements passed, praise and blame meted out, not however as utterances of Homer or Aeschylus, but as those of an Achilles or Prometheus. It is true that, even so, the poet's own hidden feelings — feelings sometimes of the most sacred nature, which he would scruple, and indeed which he would feel it a sin, to express directly — somehow find utterance: yet when a man speaks his own thoughts through another's lips modesty is observed while the agitated, full heart is

relieved.[41]

Certainly Keble did not put himself in the same category as the epic poet; but, at the same time, as a lyric poet, he believed himself consistent and sincere. For the most part, his poems show the qualities which he attributed to those written by poets of Primary rank. Apart from some of the more topical and partisan poems of *Lyra Apostolica*, this was undoubtedly so.

The *Lyra Apostolica* were originally poems contributed to *The British Magazine* anonymously apart from the designation of a Greek letter as cipher. There were 179 pieces in all: J.W. Bowden, represented as α, wrote six: Hurrell Froude, β, wrote eight: Keble as γ wrote forty-six: Newman, as δ, wrote 109: R.J. Wilberforce, as ε, wrote one; and Isaac Williams, designated ζ, wrote nine. The poems were collected and published in 1836: it was one of the books Walter Bagehot and his wife read together on honeymoon.

Keble's contributions were, on the whole, impassioned and strident: they lacked the quietness and reserve which is characteristic of most of his poetry. 'Church and King' was a Non-juring poem, a loud proclamation of England's guilt:

> Thus, when high mercy for our King we seek,
>> Back on our wincing hearts our prayers are blown
>> By our own sins, worst foes to England's throne.
> And with our own, the offences of our land
>> Too well agree to build our burthen high,
> Christ's charter blurr'd with coarse, usurping hand,
>> And gall'd with yoke of feudal tyranny
> The shoulders where the keys of David lie.

'The United States' brings that country to task for its apostasy, and its apparent dedication to the wrong causes:

> Tyre of the farther West! be thou too warn'd
>> Whose eagle wings thine own green would o'er spread,
> Touching two oceans: wherefore hast thou scorn'd
>> Thy fathers' God, O proud and full of bread?
> Why lies the Cross unhonour'd on the ground,
>> While in mid air thy stars and arrows flaunt?

In a poem of such serious address the facile rhyme and inappropriate image, of Americans 'full of bread' did little to substantiate the desired and proper effect of the poem. Keble went on to point out that, despite the fact of God's presence in the land's 'dark woods', 'forest', 'lake' and 'strand', he saw, too, that 'Mammon builds beside thy mighty floods.'

Nevertheless, the poems of *The Christian Year,* those of *Lyra Innocentium,* especially the ones similar in thought to the 'Immortality Ode', and the majority of poems in *Miscellaneous Poems,* do show most distinctly the serious expression of Keble's Christian feeling and the principles of his poetic theory. William Temple wrote that *The Christian Year,* 'is the outcome of a mind that has drunk deeply of Nature in her quieter moods, and imbibed somewhat of her power to beautify lowly things'. For Temple, Keble was particularly, 'the poet of pastoral England, the singer of green leaves and shady glades'. He wrote that reading the poems for All Saints' Day, the Twenty-fifth Sunday after Trinity, and the Fourth Sunday in Lent, is, 'like gazing at a woodland scene by Gainsborough'.

5   The Times *Obituary*

It is curious that *The Times* obituary notice,[42] on Keble's death in 1866, should have come closest, in its ironical vein, to an objective view of Keble's achievement: it stands out among the rest of Keble's admirers and eulogists. The notice allowed that the poems of *The Christian Year,* '... with all their faults, which are great, came straight from the inner soul of a good, and true, and saintly man, and they went straight to the inner soul of every hearty and honest member of the Church of England'. But it continued:

> Men read the poems, and shortly found, that without one conscious effort at learning they could say every word. An undergraduate would enter a room, seat himself at the fire, and, in a tremulous voice, pour out 'Keble' without end, receiving the faintest sign of impatience in his host with indifference, if not contempt. It was a positive possession, and soon a wide, a spreading, and a growing one. Woe to men not naturally saints or blessed with good memories!

Some lines later the obituary commented:

He ministered continually in the beautiful church he had raised out of the profits of *The Christian Year*, strangely enough, over the remains of Cromwell's family ... He found his church in the parish and the parsonage, and, perhaps we should add, the squire; but nations and great towns were out of his soundings. Very early he pronounced a great town a great evil, and held it at least a sin for a villager to seek his fortune in the wide world. It almost adds to the claims of *The Christian Year* to be a sort of Revelation, that having brought it, in an almost praeternatural manner as if from the skies, the author has done so little since ... He has written a metrical version of the psalms ... The result is useless, for any purpose except the scholar's; for the translations cannot be sung, and can hardly be read with pleasure ... But the Professor of Music had to play sad havoc with the ode (Installation of the Duke of Wellington as Vice-Chancellor) before he could set any part of it to music — much to the indignation of the author's young admirers ... But he has only done one thing — if that be to create a living thing, and a thing that shall live for generations — and that is *The Christian Year*.

The Times was certainly right about the Psalms which Keble produced: they did not live up to his hopes for them. They occupied his mind for some time. In 1835, Keble wrote to Thomas: 'Also the Abp. has sent me another note desiring to see the rest of the Psalms in M.S. and I have answered by asking a little time to revise them. I do think he is a most kind person.'[43] In 1838, an undated letter reported to his brother: 'Today, I sent the Review of Scott to N [Newman] and a letter to Parker about the Psalms. I suppose I ought to write to the Bp. of Oxford for leave to dedicate to him.'[44] A matter of a week later, according to the contents of the letter, Keble wrote again: 'The Bishop of Winton. has been very civil about the Psalms, and to reward him I think of asking leave to dedicate to him jointly with the Bp. of Oxford. But I have no answer yet from Parker about them: whereat I wonder.'[45] Perhaps Parker was as doubtful about Keble's version of the psalms as some of his critics were to be. However, on 13 March 1839, Keble told his brother more about the Psalter, and commented:

It is perplexity to find a proper title. The Oxford or Winton, or O & W Psalter, wd. do nicely, if the Prelates would allow it: but of that I have very little hope. I wish you could, some of you, think of something for me.[46]

The Psalms were not a great success. Newman passed the judgement:

His translation of the Psalms, highly valued as it is by Hebrew scholars, belongs to a department of literary labour too closely connected with grammatical science to be easily included under the term 'literature'.[47]

The Times obituary also judged correctly the Wellington Ode, but Keble had no particular illusions about that poem. He had the same difficulties as many other poets who believe in powerful inspiration, when called on to compose a poem for a specific occasion. There was no spontaneity about it, and it gave the impression of being far too contrived.

At least the writer of *The Times* notice was more discriminating and perceptive than many of Keble's apologists, and the generations which *The Christian Year* lived for were limited. It must have been a Sydney Smith, rather than a Thomas Mozley, who prepared the notice, and who felt that Keble's poetry was too much concerned with Old Testament allusion and couched in language that was rather too old-fashioned.

NOTES

1. Quotations are taken from the authorised edition, published by Parker and Company, Oxford and London, 1880. The particular copy referred to is in Keble College Library, and the text has been collated with Keble's manuscripts, in possession of the Library, by Walter Lock, 1882.
2. W.J.A. Beek, *John Keble's Literary and Religious Contribution to the Oxford Movement*, Nijmegen, 1959, p.85.
3. Joseph Butler, *Analogy*, ed. W.E. Gladstone, Oxford, 1897, p.23.
4. J.H. Newman, *Apologia*, London, 1864, p.79.
5. Butler, *Analogy*, p.34.
6. Butler, *Analogy*, Introduction, p.8.
7. C. Prince, *Leading Ideas of Keble's 'Christian Year'*, London, 1900, p.17.

8. 'The Liturgy', *Ecclesiastical Sketches*, 1822.
9. *Notes and Queries*, V, XI, p.224.
10. Coleridge, *Memoir*, Vol. II, p.321.
11. *The Christian Year*, Philadelphia, 1834.
12. *Lectures*, Vol. II, pp.432-7.
13. *Occ. Papers and Reviews*.
14. Coleridge, *Memoir*, Vol. I, p.151.
15. J. Keble, *Miscellaneous Poems*, ed. George Moberly, Oxford, 1869.
    The collection includes the 'Lyra Apostolica'.
16. J. Keble, *The Christian Year*, ed. W. Temple, London, 1875.
17. Chadwick, p.63.
18. *Tracts for the Times*, 1840, 87, p.11.
19. *Tracts*, 87, p.14.
20. *Tracts*, 87, p.16.
21. *Tracts*, 87, p.23.
22. *Tracts*, 87, p.124.
23. *Tracts*, 87, p.125.
24. *Tracts*, 89, p.22.
25. *Tracts*, 89, p.56.
26. *Tracts*, 89, p.144.
27. *Tracts*, 89, p.144.
28. *Miscellaneous Poems*, p.206.
29. *Tract*, 89, p.153.
30. *Tracts*, 89, p.155.
31. *Tracts*, 89, p.157.
32. B.M. Lott, *The Poetry of John Keble* (unpublished thesis), London
    University, 1960.
33. *Tracts*, 89, pp.185-6.
34. *Occ. Papers and Reviews*, p.17.
35. H.E.M. was, no doubt, Harriet Elizabeth Mozley, J.H. Newman's
    sister who married Thomas Mozley in 1836. Thomas Mozley was
    a clergyman, and a Fellow of Oriel College: he edited *The British
    Critic* 1841-3, and was a leader writer for *The Times*, 1844.
36. E.N.S. Thompson, *The Temple and The Christian Year*, PMLA,
    Vol. 54, 1939, pp.1081-25.
37. *Lectures*, Vol. II, p.99.
38. Correspondence, C15.
39. A.H. Warren, *English Poetic Theory, 1825-1865*, 1966, p.65.
40. Abrams, pp.21-2.
41. *Lectures*, Vol. II, p.97.
42. The writer is unknown: there are no records of who wrote
    obituaries in *The Times* prior to 1894. Keble's obituary
    appeared in the paper on 6 April, p.5, col. 1.
43. Correspondence, C14.
44. Correspondence, C14.
45. Correspondence, C14.
46. Correspondence, C14.
47. *Occ. Papers and Reviews*, p.xii.

Conclusion

As it turned out, J.S. Rowntree's prediction that Keble and his poetry would be subjects for examination papers of the future, proved erroneous; and *The Times*'s prognostication that *The Christian Year* would live for generations was not fulfilled. The last accolades for *The Christian Year* came with its publication in the 'World's Classics' series in 1901, and in 'Everyman's Library' in 1906 and 1914. Otherwise, the immense popularity of Keble's poetry has waned.

The reason for the decline is, ironically enough, because his poetry showed a most successful assimilation of his religious and aesthetic thought; and, as shown in the preceding analyses and commentaries, the very clear relationship between his poetry, his Christianity and his literary theory, made him, above all, a religious, and therefore restricted, poet. The nineteenth century, which was notable for a grand effusion of religious poetry, celebrated the best examples: Keble's poems consequently excelled: they were eminently acceptable to the mass of the Victorian middle class for what they offered in the way of comfort and consolation. As Keble wrote in the Advertisement to *The Christian Year*, '... in times of much leisure and unbounded curiosity, when excitement of every kind is sought after with a morbid eagerness', the aim of his poems was to supplement the 'soothing tendency of the Prayer Book'. This, his poetic audience appreciated, and it took to his poems, and those of other religious poets, in the face of uncertainties and doubts being cast by rational philosophers and scientists. His poetry appealed, like Tennyson's 'In Memoriam', to people who were disconcerted by the Evolutionists. In Tennyson's words:

> ... They say,
> The solid earth whereon we tread
> In tracts of fluent heat began,
>   And grew to seeming-random forms,
>   And seeming prey of cyclic storms,
> Till at the least arose the man.[1]

The religious poets gave reassurance and spiritual comfort to people in a world of developing scientific thought which they did not understand and which they were frightened to countenance.

Keble, foremost among those nineteenth-century religious poets fulfilled the need for the great majority of people; but the fact that his poetry was essentially Christian was its own limitation. Religious poetry is intense, concentrated and demanding: it is also narrow, and not necessarily universal. So, Keble's poetry did not live long into an age in which most people were indifferent to Christianity. Dame Helen Gardner has pointed out that nowadays a religious poet has to meet a problem of communication which did not exist for him in earlier centuries: 'Words and symbols that lay to hand for earlier writers as sure to evoke a universal response have lost their power.'[2] It is this process which has made Keble's poetry more esoteric than even he would have wished. Naturally, the poets of his own period were affected by him, especially through *The Christian Year*. The general currency and availability of his poetry in the nineteenth century are indications of its irrefutable influence. Wordsworth's later poetry came under Keble's influence, with not any very good outcome; and some of Tennyson's poetry shows signs of Old Testament allusion and imagery which may have had their origin in Keble's poetry. For instance, parts of 'In Memoriam' show this:

> And Power was with him in the night,
> Which makes the darkness and the light,
> And dwells not in the light alone,
> But in the darkness and the cloud,
> As over Sinai's peaks of old,
> While Israel made their gods of gold,
> Altho' the trumpet blew so loud.[3]

However now, when people are not familiar with the Church of England's formularies and do not know its liturgy, it is impossible for Keble's poetry to live on in the popular mind.

Nonetheless, Keble's words and symbols were interesting in that they formed a bridge between old ideas and new ones which were to appear later in the century. In fact Keble's isolation as a religious poet is not so complete as it might seem. His conservatism, his classical and therefore conventional thought, led him back to the great authors of Greece and Rome, as well as to the great poets of England, such as Spenser, and he made use of their ideas in a way which was to show promise of poets to come. His use of symbolism is an example of this, and so is his idea of reserve, the veil hiding the truth until such time as it is able to be properly understood. The poet disguising his personal feelings in the poetic form from the vulgar glare of publicity, gives promise of a later symbolism by which the poet hides behind a *persona* or a mask. Keble, had, in a sense, prepared the way for Romanticism to progress into Symbolism. John Bayley has shown how, towards the end of the nineteenth century, poets began to reject poetry as a criticism of life and, in Yeats's words, were 'convinced that it is a revelation of a hidden life': Bayley wrote that the poet's claim became:

> ...his ability to initiate the chosen into the great secret, which, though all-embracing, is mysterious and only to be understood by the few. As Schure modestly put it in *Les Grands Initiés:* 'La doctrine esotérique n'est pas seulement une science, une philosophie, une morale, une religion — elle est la science, la philosophie ... 'and so forth.[4]

Antiquated, and yet strangely modern, such were Keble's ideas; and what has been ignored is that they were original in nineteenth-century criticism. In fact, it is as a literary critic that Keble should have his more permanent reputation. Although Matthew Arnold dominated the critical stage in the latter half of the nineteenth century, it is little realised how much his ideas owe to Keble. The Professor who succeeded to the Chair of Poetry in 1857 at the age of thirty-five, and who lectured before his Oxford audience for the first time in English, owed much to the Professor of the years 1832-41. It is interesting to note that Keble's personal library contains both Arnold's Poems and *Essays in Criticism* which were presented to Keble by their author and inscribed by him.

In Arnold's criticism, as in Keble's, there is a certain degree of intellectual and academic arrogance. The English romantics, on the whole, in comparison with the French, or the Germans like Goethe — simply did not know enough. He roundly attacked the criminal complacency and insularity of English society, in much the same way that Keble did on many occasions; and like Keble, too, Arnold advocated the propagation and dissemination of 'the best that is known and thought in the world'.

Perhaps more important than anything else was Arnold's debt to Keble in the matter of biographical criticism. Keble had looked closely at what was able to be learned about the sort of life which poets such as Homer, Theocritus and Virgil, had led: obviously, their quality of life bore a strict relationship to the quality of their poetry. This was also true of his contemporary poets, which was the reason that he censured both Shelley and Byron. It should be remembered that Keble reproached them both in the poem for Palm Sunday, and called on them to do better things:

> Mount, and claim your glorious meed;
> Linger not with sin and woe.

Arnold developed a similar approach in biographical criticism, combined with ideas of works possessing a high degree of moral seriousness.

Similarly, Arnold owed a great deal to Keble in the matter of the relationship between poetry and religion. George Watson has written that both Eliot and Lionel Trilling have been wrong in suggesting that Arnold ever sought to substitute poetry for religion: he pointed out that the misunderstanding rested on a key passage in *The Study of Poetry* (1880): 'Without poetry, our science will appear incomplete; and most of what now passes with us for religion and philosophy will be replaced by poetry.' Watson drew attention to the words, 'what now passes with us for religion', and went on to say: 'It is the sham religion of dogmatic assertion which will be replaced by poetry, not the true religion of Christian humanism.'[5] Although Keble would not have agreed with all that Arnold said, nevertheless the idea was Keble's. So was Arnold's elaboration that poetry and religion are twin currents in the flow of existence, and that he saw their relationship as one of analogy.

Yet not only Arnold's criticism shows the marks of Keble's thought, but Ruskin's does too. For example, Ruskin's Preface to *A Joy for Ever,* written in 1880, expressed much of what Keble felt about aesthetics, especially the value of local influence in helping to constitute a work of art:

> ... for there never was, nor can be, any essential beauty possessed by a work of art, which is not based on the conception of its honoured permanence, and local influence, as a part of appointed and precious furniture, either in the cathedral, the house, or the joyful thoroughfare, of nations which enter their gates with thanksgiving, and their courts with praise.

Keble, Arnold and Ruskin all thought that there should be an interdependence of art and the age in which it was produced; it seems, now, as though the principle were part of a common Victorian ideal.

Keble's great caution in seeking to avoid what might be new and therefore disturbing or even shocking led him back to the ancients; but in doing so he discovered old truths, which both in the practice and theory of poetry, others took and developed. With no intention on his part, he became a precursor. M.H. Abrams, commenting on the structure of Keble's *Lectures on Poetry,* drew attention to the surprising qualities of Keble's ideas on poetic composition acting in a purging and medicinal way on the overwrought poet's mind (see p. 92ff.) Abrams wrote about the Lectures:

> They broach views of the source, the function and the effect of literature, and of the methods by which literature is appropriately read and criticised, which, when they occur in the writings of critics schooled by Freud, are still reckoned to be the most subversive to the established values and principles of literary criticism.[6]

Keble had no intention of being subversive, of course: nothing was further from his mind; but he did recognise that there was a serious conflict between emotions needing positively to express themselves, and a feeling of reticence or shame which forbade revelation. The solution was to give expression of the powerful emotions at the same time as maintaining a 'modest reserve' by way of certain veils and disguises. This process Abrams described as 'a proto-Freudian theory' which conceived 'literature as disguised wish-fulfillment' saving the poet from imminent neurosis. His final analysis was that: 'Ideas, which in theology have become matter of course and inert, may become alive and drastically innovative when transferred — as Keble patently transferred them — into the soil of aesthetics.'[7]

In the time that has passed in just over a hundred years since Keble's death, his position in literature has become more clear. As a critic, he was learned, strict and moralistic, encouraging the practical task of looking at traces left in poetry for evidence of the sentiments and temperament of the poet who wrote it. His theories have been elaborated and developed.

As a poet, however, his fame has been limited largely to his own century perhaps because of both Dr Johnson's strictures against religious poetry, and Helen Gardner's diagnosis. Helen Gardner's comments on the problem of communication which a religious poet eventually runs into has been true of Keble's fate. Dr Johnson's objections are trenchant but less certain: indeed, Keble argued carefully against them in his review 'Sacred Poetry'.[8] Keble took most of the points which Helen Gardner has raised from Johnson's criticism in his life of Waller and answered them in detail. For instance Keble wrote:

> He [Johnson] argues the point, first, from the nature of poetry, and afterwards from that of devotion.
>
> 'The essence of poetry is invention; such invention as, by producing something unexpected, surprises and delights. The topics of devotion are few.'
>
> It is to be hoped that many men's experience will refute the latter part of this statement. How can the topics of devotion be few, when we are taught to make every part of life, every scene in nature, an occasion — in other words, a topic — of devotion? It might as well be said that connubial love is an unfit subject for poetry, as being incapable of novelty, because, after all, it is only ringing

the changes upon one simple affection, which everyone understands.[9]

And a little further on he quoted Johnson again: "'Whatever is great, desirable, or tremendous, is comprised in the name of the Supreme Being. Omnipotence cannot be exalted; infinity cannot be amplified; perfection cannot be improved.'" Keble remarked:

> True: all perfection is implied in the Name of God; and so all the beauties and luxuries of spring are comprised in that one word. But is it not the very office of poetry to develop and display the particulars of such complex ideas? in such a way, for example, as the idea of God's omnipresence is developed in the 139th Psalm?[10]

However, in the final analysis, although it is possible for a man of Keble's intellectual calibre to attack and sometimes refute the details of Johnson's argument, the body of it remains; and the readers of poetry are left agreeing with T.S. Eliot when he states that:

> For the great majority of people who love poetry, '*religious poetry*' is a variety of *minor* poetry: the religious poet is not a poet who is treating the whole subject matter of poetry in a religious spirit, but a poet who is dealing with a confined part of this subject matter: who is leaving out what men consider their major passions, and thereby confessing his ignorance of them.[11]

Eliot's judgement on religious poetry is the final judgement on Keble: although he appealed greatly to the people of his day, in the end he survives as a minor poet, because he confines himself to a particular sort of poetry. No matter how much Keble would have protested intellectually, and privately not publicly, against this judgement, his very success in relating his religious and aesthetic thought to his poetry, ensured his eventual reputation. The priest and the professor became one in the poet: the priest and poet became one in the professor: the professor has endured longer and better than the poet.

NOTES

1. Lord Tennyson, *In Memoriam*, CXVIII.
2. Helen Gardner, *Religion and Literature*, London, 1971, p.137.
3. *In Memoriam*, XCVI.
4. J.O. Bayley, *The Romantic Survival*, London, 1957, p.43.
5. G. Watson, *The Literary Critics*, London, 1962, p.157.
6. Abrams, p.145.
7. Abrams, p.147.
8. *Occ. Papers and Reviews*.
9. *Occ. Papers and Reviews*, p.92.
10. *Occ. Papers and Reviews*, p.94.
11. T.S. Eliot, 'Religion and Literature', *Essays Ancient and Modern*, London, 1936, p.97.

Appendix A

Keble's attitudes towards social and political problems are clearly shown in his letters to his brother Thomas. His views were, without doubt, conservative, but his remarks cast light on issues important in his time and absolve him from the charge of being unaware of the real conditions of society. The following extracts from letters to his brother kept in Keble College Library, together with extracts quoted in footnote 17 on p. 118 are evidence of this.

I have just read the Commons' Report on the Poor Laws, and am quite delighted with it — but much fear nothing will be done.

Undated, 1817. (C13)

A committee has been appointed in 1817 to consider Poor Law reform, but the recommendations were not very positive and, as Keble feared, little came of it.)

... persuaded me to stop and see what Wadham does, i.e. to wait till next Monday or so, by which time we conclude that their majesty the mob, who are reported to be settling matters their own way about Swindon, will either have paid us a visit or have gone quite out of the way ... The farmers have been knocking their machines to pieces, and agreeing to raise the wages of labour, and Mr Barker has been lowering his rent accordingly. So if there is any row here, it must be mere wantonness. Mr Brown is taking similar measures at Coln.

Undated, no year: most likely 1831. (C14)

... The worst is, our Farmers and Magistrates are coward and have given in, and these fellows have got higher wages to reward them for breaking the machines.

Undated, no year: possibly 1831. (C14)

Mr Morrell talked to me very much about your poor people, and would be most glad to give more himself, and to patronize a subscription in Oxford, if you wish it: only he thinks in the latter case there should be a statement drawn up of some of the details. I wish I knew what your Farmers pay for rates in the pound per annum.

October 1834. (C14)

Also you must look to your weights and measures, for they are busy stamping them all the country over (N.B. The Whigs have past an act for stamping *cast Iron weights which will take no stamp.*)

Undated, 1834. (C14)

This place is in dudgeon high about the workhouse, and we hear disagreeable reports about dirt and unkindness in the management of it, which is very unlucky at first setting out. Our Squire after promising to be quiet is just setting out at the head of his tenantry to join the attack on the Church unless this ringing and firing is a sign that the garrison has surrendered.

Undated: Monday Morning, 1835. (C14)

I have got some garden Allotments and expect to have some applications for them tomorrow. From what I can hear the folk will be just as well satisfied whether they are permitted to grow corn or no. I shall *not* allow it this year: especially considering that Sir Bob [Sir Robert Peel] is going to keep up the Malt Tax.

Undated, 1835. (C14)

Our Farmers here speak very badly of the Wheat, chiefly on account of that violent wind which they say blew off the blossoms ... The travelling on Sundays on this railroad is disgusting; they quite disturb the people in Otterburn Church.

24 July 1839. (C14)

Appendix B

In the course of reading manuscripts in Keble College Library, two pieces of writing in particular have seemed to shed new light on Keble's appearance and character.

The first, unpublished, is an extract from the journal of the Reverend Kilvert written in October 1822. Robert Kilvert was the father of the famous diarist, and was an undergraduate at Oriel, a pupil of Hawkins, but a member of Keble's lecture class. In his journal, he described his arrival at Oriel with a letter of introduction to Keble, and went on to describe his experiences. The extract in Keble College Library has been photocopied and supplied by D.T.W. Price. Part of it reads:

> ... Of Keble I have many pleasant recollections altho' he continued Tutor only during my first two terms. He was a small dark man, most unimposing in appearance and undemonstrative in manner and speech — the tones of his speech — the tones of his voice rather rough and unmusical — very short-sighted, without any, even the most distant, approach to assumption or self-assertion — and yet commanding a degree of respect and even reverence, such as is rarely met with. I never heard of the wildest undergraduate with any of the feelings of a gentleman taking the smallest liberty with him. I have seen men who were ass to anything in the way of frolic and irregularity, subdued to a perfect decorum of manner at his lectures — not taking advantage of his imperfect eyesight, or returning even an aside or whispered remark. This may have been partly owing to the high reputation he had achieved at a very early age for talent and excellence of character. But besides this, there was a nameless waft of simple goodness about him, the presence, as it were of an unsullied childlike nature which put to shame all indelicacy or irreverence. It is astonishing too what an amount of pleasure would be caused by even the smallest note of approbation from him. I remember to this day the thrill of

gratification when he came in at lecture time from an inner room with a number of papers in his hand, and looking round the class assembled, with his short-sighted peering glance, singled me out and tossed my exercise to me with a smile. It was more to me than a laudatory speech from anyone else.

The second is a letter written by Keble to Thomas, his brother, sent from Romsey and dated 28 November (C14). Georgina Battiscombe, in her biography of Keble, quoted part of the letter, but much of it has not been published. She used her extracts to prove points about Newman's character; and certainly the letter does give interesting evidence for a study of his temperament. More important is the evidence which it lends for the drawing of Keble's character: it shows his willingness, and resolution, to stand by Newman at a time when Newman was being attacked by his friends over the content of the Tract concerning the translation of the Breviary. The letter shows, too, Keble's ability to mediate, and smooth the troubled waters which had arisen between the Bisley School and Newman at Oxford. And it shows, perhaps above all, Keble's characteristic self-effacement, whether calculated or natural, and his modesty — noticeable throughout his life. The *Remains* referred to are Hurrell Froude's which Newman and Keble edited: the first part in two volumes was published in 1838; the second part in two volumes was published in 1839. The greater part of the letter to Thomas reads:

I want you to consider whether you and Prevost and Jeffreys are quite doing justice to Newman, in the sort of exceptions which for some time past (I think ever since the Remains) you have made about his proceedings. You have talked generally about not trusting him — about going a rail-road pace etc. But when particular points were mentioned you avoided any discussion of them, I mean any statement of what you would think right: and at the same time you deprecated the notion of giving up the Tracts. This rather hurts and embarrasses him — he feels as if he was looked with suspicion [*sic*], without any frank and quiet explanation of the cause, and declares that it is so painful to him that he thinks he could not go on writing with that sort of suspicion on his mind. He puts himself entirely in my hands, of to stop the Tracts entirely, to put an end to his Tuesday evening parties or anything else which I recommend. In particular he mentions that it is his rule to show his writing to some one or other before publication. Pusey saw [illegible] , Williams heard the last Tract and gave his Imprimatur to it. This being so, he hopes he may be treated with confidence, and have the best interpretation put on what he says, unless it is wished to stop him altogether. This, I think, is the substance of his letter. I told him in reply what I think — that you P and J. do not in my opinion make quite sufficient allowances for his very difficult situation; I did not add, what I suppose is true, that such very clever persons must submit to be misconstrued by us middling ones. I told him he was naturally very sensitive (which he is to an extreme) and I thought he would perceive on reflection that nothing unfriendly could be intended ... You will naturally say, 'well, if he is so touchy I will fast leave off admonishing him altogether', but I do not think in fact you will say it, because you know too well what sort of a person he really is. I feel for him extremely and the more because in general he is so reserved about his own feelings that one supposes nothing but strong pressure would make him cry out in this way. Something or other in Prevost's letter must have been greatly misconstrued by him. I did not see it; and now rather wish I had. I have been again looking over this last Tract and cannot see how it tends to Romanism except in comparison to Latitudinism ... Whatever strikes you as blameable in his books, perhaps for some little time to come you had better bring your objections to my shop, and I will promise to deal more civilly with them than I have sometimes done, I fear, and if I think best I will state them fairly and quietly to him. I wish he was not so keen in his feelings; but I suppose it goes along with his keeness of perception: I have observed it in him always at times, but he veils it wonderfully. I saw nothing of it whilst I was staying with him in Oxford, it all came out in a letter since.

Bibliography

I *The Writings of John Keble (1792—1866)*

A chronological list is published in W. Beek's *John Keble's Contribution to the Oxford Movement*, Nijmegen, 1959, which is based on Walter Lock's list published in *John Keble*, London, 1895. My researches prove the list to be authoritative with the exception of the 1831 entry 'A hint from Bristol', which has been impossible to locate.

II *Manuscripts*

1. Keble College Library. Much of the Keble family correspondence is kept in a series of envelopes and boxes. The letters of John Keble to his brother Thomas are of particular importance. (For Keble College's method of cataloguing the letters, see footnote 9, p. 21.) Keble's letters to Newman, presented to the College by Newman and also censored by Newman, are among the papers.
2. Lambeth Palace Library. The Reverend Canon Edward Keble's collection of papers are on permanent loan to the Palace Library. Deposit 2 contains letters of John Keble, and letters written to him. There is now no Keble family correspondence at Fairford apart from one framed letter of Newman.
3. Small collections of letters in the possession of Corpus Christi College, Oriel College, the Bodleian Library, the British Museum and the National Library of Scotland.

III *Works relating particularly to John Keble*
(Unless otherwise stated, the place of publication is London.)

1. *Books*
Battiscombe, G., *John Keble*, 1963.
Beek, W.J.A.M., *John Keble's Literary and Religious Contribution to the Oxford Movement*, Nijmegen, 1959.
Coleridge, Sir J.T., *A Memoir of the Rev. J. Keble*, 3rd ed., Oxford, 1870.
Concordance to 'The Christian Year', Oxford and London, 1871.

Lock, W., *John Keble, A Biography*, 7th ed., 1895.

MacKarness, C., *The Poetry of Keble as a guide to the clergy in their pastoral work*, ed. W. Lock, 1918.

Price, C., *Leading Ideas of Keble's Christian Year*, 1890.

Shairp, J.C., *Keble and the Christian Year*, Edinburgh, 1866.

Warren, W.T., *Kebleland*, Winchester, 1900.

Wood, E.F.L., 'John Keble', in *Leaders of the Church, 1800 – 1900*, 1909.

Yonge, C.M., *Musings over the Christian Year and Lyra Innocentium*, Oxford, 1871.

Unpublished Thesis:

Lott, B.M., 'The Poetry of John Keble, with special reference to *The Christian Year* and his contribution to *Lyra Apostolica*', London University, 1960.

2. *Sermons and Articles*

Churton, E., 'The power of holy minstrelsy', sermon preached after the funeral of John Keble, 1866 (Bodleian Library).

McCheane, J.H., 'In quietness and confidence shall be your strength', sermon after the burial of John Keble, Leeds, 1866.

Richards, J.W., 'He being dead yet speaketh', a sermon after the burial of John Keble, Salisbury, 1866 (unpublished), Bodleian Library.

Thompson, E.N.S., *The Temple and The Christian Year*, PMLA, Vol. 54, 1939.

Rowntree, J., 'Notes on the Christian Year', *Friends' Quarterly Examiner*, reprint, Bodleian Library, 1927.

IV *Background and General*
(Unless otherwise stated, the place of publication is London.)

1. *Publications by Keble's predecessors, contemporaries, and by other nineteenth-century writers*

Arnold, M., *Essays in Criticism*, 1865.

Poems, ed. K. Allott, 1965.

Barbauld, Mrs, *Hymns in Prose for Children*, 1781.

Bunyan, J., *Book for Boys and Girls*, 1686.

Burgon, J.W., *Lives of Twelve Good Men*, 1888.

Burke, Edmund, *The works of*, 1899.

Church, R.W., *The Oxford Movement, 1833-45*, 1892.

Coleridge, S.T., *Biographia Literaria*, Everyman, 1934.

Fathers, Library of, ed. E.B. Pusey, and others, Oxford, 1838-85.

Froude, J.A., *Short Studies on Great Subjects, Selections*, Fontana, 1963.

Froude, R.H., *Remains*, 1838-39.

Gladstone, W.E., *The Works of Butler*, Oxford, 1896. *Studies subsidiary to the Works of Bishop Butler*, (Oxford, 1896).

Kingsley, C., *Yeast*, 1851.

Liddon, H.P., *Life of E.B. Pusey*, 1894.

Miles, A.H., *Poets of the Century* (Sacred, Moral and Religious Verse), 1891-97.

Mozley, T.B., *Reminiscences chiefly of Oriel College, and the Oxford Movement*, 1882.

Newman, J.H., *Apologia Pro Vita Sua and Newman's and Kingsley's pamphlets*, ed. W. Ward, Oxford, 1913. *Correspondence of J.H. Newman with John Keble and Others, 1839-49*, ed. at Birmingham Oratory, 1917. *Essay in aid of a Grammar of Assent, An*, 1913.

Newman, J.H., *Idea of a University Defined and Illustrated*, The, 1873. *Letters and Diaries of J.H. Newman*, ed. Dessain, 1961. *Loss and Gain*, 1848. *Parochial and Plain Sermons*, 1878.

Oakley, F., *Personal Reminiscences of the Oxford Movement*, 1855.

Pattison, M., *Memoirs*, 1885.

Prevost, G., (ed.), *The Autobiography of Isaac Williams*, 1892.

Shairp, J.C., *Studies in Poetry and Philosophy*, Oxford, 1881.

Tracts for the Times, by members of the University of Oxford, Oxford and London, 1833-40.

Ward, W., *W.G. Ward and the Oxford Movement*, 1889.

Watts, Isaac, *Divine and Moral Songs*, 1715.

Wordsworth, W., and Coleridge, S.T., *Lyrical Ballads*, 1798.

Wordsworth, W., and Coleridge, S.T., *Lyrical Ballads*, 1800.
Wordsworth, W., and Coleridge, S.T., *Lyrical Ballads*, 1802.

2. *Twentieth century publications, relevant to Keble's religious thought*

Bindoff, S.T., *Tudor England*, Penguin, 1950.
Cameron, J.M., *J.H. Newman*, British Council, 1956.
Chadwick, H., *The Early Church*, Penguin, 1967.
Chadwick, O., *The Mind of the Oxford Movement*, 1960.
  The Reformation, Penguin, 1964.
  The Victorian Church, 1970.
Chapman, R., *Faith and Revolt. Studies in the Literary Influences of the Oxford Movement*, 1970.
Cockshut, A.O.J., *Anglican Attitudes*, 1959.
Danielou, and others, *Pelican Guide to Modern Theology*, Vol. 2, Penguin, 1962.
Dawson, C., *The Spirit of the Oxford Movement*, 1933.
Elliot-Binns, L.E., *Religion in the Victorian Era*, London and Redhill, 1936.
Faber, G., *Oxford Apostles*, Penguin, 1954.
Fathers of the Church, ed. Schopp and others, Washington, 1947.
Fathers, Early Christian, A Selection from, ed. Bettenson, Oxford, 1969.
Jones, O.W., *Isaac Williams and his Circle*, 1971.
Kitson-Clark, G., *The Making of Victorian England*, 1962.
Matthieson, W.L., *English Church Reform 1815-40*, 1923.
Neil, S., *Anglicanism*, Penguin, 1958.
Newsome, D., *The Parting of Friends*, 1966.
Storr, V.R., *The Development of English Theology in the Nineteenth Century, 1800-1860*, 1913.
Stranks, C.J., *Anglican Devotion*, 1961.
Symondson, A. (ed.), *The Victorian Crisis of Faith*, 1970.
Ward, W., *The Life of J.H., Cardinal Newman*, 1913.
Webb, C.C.J., *Religious Thought in the Oxford Movement*, 1928.
Woodward, E.L., *The Age of Reform*, 6th ed., Oxford, 1954.
Young, G.M., *Victorian England*, Oxford, 1936.

3. *Twentieth century publications, relevant to Keble's aesthetic thought*

Abrams, M.H., *The Mirror and the Lamp* (Norton Library) Oxford, 1958.

Bayley, J.O., *The Romantic Survival*, 1957.

Cambridge History of English Literature, The, Cambridge, 1953.

Cruse, Amy, *The Victorians and their Books*, 1935.

Eliot, T.S., 'Religion and Literature', *Essays Ancient and Modern*, 1936.

Faber, R., *Proper Stations: Class in Victorian Fiction*, 1971.

Gardner, H., *Religion and Literature*, 1971.

Maison, M.M., *Search Your Soul Eustace*, 1961.

Mare, M., and Percival, A.C., *Victorian Best-Seller*, 1947.

Moorman, M., *William Wordsworth: A Biography*, Oxford, 1965.

Pollard, A., *English Hymns*, British Council, 1960.

Warren, A.H., *English Poetic Theory, 1825-65*, Princeton, 1950.

Watson, G., *The Literary Critics*, Penguin, 1962.

Willey, B., *Nineteenth Century Studies*, 1949.

Wimsatt, W.K., and Brooks, C., *Literary Criticism, A Short History*, Vol. III, 1957.

Index

188